CISTERCIAN FATHERS SERIES: NUMBER FIFTY-SEVEN

Walter Daniel

The Life of Aelred of Rievaulx

D1553486

CISTERCIAN FATHERS SERIES: NUMBER FIFTY-SEVEN

The Life of Aelred of Rievaulx

by

Walter Daniel

Translated from the Latin and annotated by

F.M. Powicke

Introduction by

Marsha Dutton

Cistercian Publications
Kalamazoo, Michigan — Spencer, Massachusetts

The work of Cistercian Publications is made possible in part
by support from Western Michigan University to
The Institute of Cistercian Studies

TABLE OF CONTENTS

Introduction to Walter Daniel's *Vita Aelredi*   7

The Life or Aelred by Walter Daniel   89

Lament for Aelred   140

Walter Daniels' *Letter to Maurice*   147

Notes to The Life of Aelred   159

Notes to the Lament   170

Notes to The Letter to Maurice   171

Introduction to
Walter Daniel's *Vita Aelredi**

OUR FATHER IS DEAD; he has vanished from our
world like the morning sunshine, and many hearts long
that this great life should flood with its brightness the
memory of generations to come, and indeed of those still living
for whom it shone in all its splendor.

So Walter Daniel begins his prefatory letter to his Life of
Aelred, third abbot of the english cistercian abbey of Rievaulx,
introducing the work that follows as a eulogy and commemoration
of his beloved abbot and friend. That work, which apparently
appeared soon after Aelred's death on 12 January 1167, portrays
Aelred as a man of wisdom, humility, charity, and sanctity, set
apart by his love for God and his spiritual sons at Rievaulx.
Walter portrays a man characterized by 'charity and astonishing
sanctity' (1) rather than giving an historical account of Aelred,
twelfth-century northumbrian and cistercian monk. He provides
what Thomas Heffernan calls *sacred biography*, 'a narrative text of

---

*I am, as always, grateful to Frank Luttmer and Father M. John-Baptist
Porter, ocso, for their assistance to me in the writing and editing of these pages.
David Voelker has been especially generous in reading my pages and advising me,
pointing out verbal flaws, repetitiveness, logical contradictions, and, too rarely,
insights and felicitous phrasings. I do thank him. Finally, I want to acknowledge
all that I owe to Charles L. Flynn, Jr., through whom I have come at last to
understand Aelred's life and Walter's response to it.

7

the *vita* of the saint written by a member of a community of belief'.[1]

Walter Daniel, a monk at Rievaulx during Aelred's abbacy, appears to have written the *Vita* at the request of a certain Abbot H, at least in part to ward off criticism that Aelred was ambitious, overly involved in public affairs, and altogether too much a man of the world beyond Rievaulx and the Cistercian Order. Walter's desire to show Aelred's sanctity through his exemplary charity, his life of prayer and contemplation, and his gentle guidance of his spiritual sons, along with Walter's concern to defend Aelred's memory against those who would criticize his activity outside the monastery, means that Aelred the diplomat, arbitrator, popular guest preacher, and adviser and friend of kings is difficult to discern in the *Vita*. Walter's deep admiration and love for his abbot and his efforts to convey the reasons for that admiration and love have powerfully preserved the memory of the private Aelred, monk, abbot, and spiritual guide, a man of patience, humility, charity, gentle counsel, and spiritual power.

MEDIEVAL LIVES OF AELRED

The *Vita Aelredi* survives in a single manuscript from Jesus College, Cambridge, MS Q.B. 7 (ff. 63v-74r); M. R. James dates it to the late fourteenth century, 'most likely from Durham'. In the manuscript it follows Walter Daniel's 'Letter to Maurice', written soon after the *Vita* in response to criticisms of the earlier work, and precedes a brief hitherto untranslated Lament for Aelred.[2]

---

[1]Thomas J. Heffernan, *Sacred Biography: Saints and their Biographers in the Middle Ages* (New York: Oxford UP, 1988) p. 15. Heffernan uses this term, rather than 'hagiography' or 'saint's life', noting that the former term 'is now virtually impossible to read except as an epithet signifying a pious fiction or an exercise in panegyric'. His discussion of the distinctions between the *sacred biography* of the patristic and medieval periods and modern, *empirical biography*, with its dependence on documentary sources and attempt to reconstruct the external events of its subject's life, is most helpful; see pp. 15–18, 39–49. I have been greatly assisted by Heffernan's analysis of changing modes in and expectations of biography and by his careful study of the *Vita Aelredi* in the third chapter of his book, pp. 72–122.

[2]M. R. James, *A Descriptive Catalogue of the Manuscripts in the Library of Jesus College, Cambridge* (London: Clay, 1895) pp. 28–29. James identifies the Lament, which remains unpublished, on f. 74r-v, as 'Lamentacio auctoris vite eiusdem

Although the *Vita* and the Letter to Maurice were first edited and translated in 1950 by Sir Maurice Powicke,[3] earlier authors had conflated materials from the two to create their own lives of Aelred. In the second quarter of the fourteenth century John of Tynemouth, a monk at Saint Alban's, composed a new Life for inclusion in his *Sanctilogium Angliae*; his version was revised by John Capgrave, printed in Wynkyn de Worde's *Nova Legenda Angliae* in 1516, and reprinted by the Bollandists in the *Acta Sanctorum* in 1643. Another Life, which also incorporates materials from both the *Vita* and the Letter, survives in a late fourteenth-century manuscript from Bury Saint Edmund's, now Bodleian MS Bodley 240. Carl Horstmann published both versions in 1901.[4]

WALTER DANIEL

In selecting Walter Daniel to write Aelred's Life, Abbot H chose a man who had not only known Aelred long and well but who was a scholar and already an established writer. Walter had spent seventeen years at Rievaulx during Aelred's abbacy and was familiar with the intimate details of the abbot's life during his last decade. He identifies himself in the *Vita* as Aelred's scribe (27) and refers in the Lament to his service to Aelred *in officio medicus*.[5] While these words need not mean that he was the monastic infirmarian, his detailed discussion of Aelred's various illnesses and of the symptoms of some of the people Aelred miraculously healed shows his knowledge about and interest in human illness and its treatment. Of all the monks who sat and talked for hours at the abbot's bedside, Walter seems to have been the most regularly there, storing up all he saw and heard for his own memories

---

de eadem re'; it begins 'In exordio in processu et in fine lamentacionis mee ne ridiculus appaream.'

[3]Sir Maurice Powicke, *The Life of Ailred of Rievaulx by Walter Daniel* (1950; Oxford: Clarendon, 1978), Introduction, p. xi. I am indebted to the late Sir Maurice's invaluable work, which has assisted me immeasurably. His translation follows.

[4]Carl Horstmann, ed., *Nova Legenda Angliae* (Oxford: Oxford Univ. Press, 1901) 1.ix, 1vii–1ix. Both medieval versions are contained in this edition, the Capgrave Life at 1.41–46 and the Bury MS Life at 2.544–53.

[5]Powicke, p. xxvii: *Et licet mihi sim in officio medicus, non tamen sine acerbo dolore curo. Sed nunc cura certa huius artis constat, que pendet e medicina remota a corpore.*

and for narratives to tell and retell in later years. The *Vita* gives a powerful sense of Walter's constant presence at Aelred's side; while others come and go, Walter's eye and voice are always there.

Besides knowing Aelred in his last years better than almost anyone else, Walter was surely the most prolific writer at Rievaulx other than Aelred himself. Although the medieval catalogue of Rievaulx does not record a copy of the *Vita Aelredi* or the Lament, it lists nine of Walter's other works: *Centum sententiae, Centum homiliae, Epistolae, De virginitate Mariae, Expositio super Missus est angelus Gabriel, De honesta virginitatis formula, De onere jumentorum austri, De vera amicitia,* and *De conceptione beatae Mariae.* Only the first of these seems to have survived, in a manuscript from Rievaulx, but four of Walter's sermons also appear in that manuscript.[6] Abbot H would have been hard put to find a better choice to write the book of Aelred's life.

The *Vita* offers some slight insight into its author's personal history. Walter's claim that he was at Rievaulx with Aelred for seventeen years (40) means that he must have entered in 1150. And his statement that it was Aelred 'who begot me to the life of Saint Benedict through the Gospel of God' (2) suggests that he may have been brought into monastic life through Aelred's influence, perhaps meeting the abbot while on a visit to his father, who was apparently a monk at Rievaulx by 1147.

The father, whom Walter identifies twice in the *Vita* as 'the lord Daniel my father', was apparently one of ten Rievaulx monks sent to Swineshead Abbey, a former savigniac house in Lincolnshire, 'to illuminate it with the cistercian way of life' (35). That mission must have taken place around 1147, when all the houses of Savigny came into the Cistercian Order. Powicke suggests that *dominus Daniel* may have been 'of knightly origin', perhaps from the Balliol fief in Cleveland.[7]

The combined evidence of the titles of Walter's works and the range of his learning in philosophy, theology, medicine, and

[6]For a discussion of Walter Daniel's works, see Powicke, pp. xvii–xxvi. See also David N. Bell, *An Index of Authors and Works in Cistercian Libraries in Great Britain,* CS 130 (Kalamazoo: Cistercian, 1992) p. 145.
[7]Powicke, p. xlii.

rhetoric revealed by his lengthy digressions in the *Vita* indicate that he had received a formal education before entering Rievaulx. Powicke was of the opinion that while Walter may have studied at Oxford or Paris, his schooling was more likely local.[8] Some glimpse of his learning appears in his rhetorical use of mathematical relationships: he sometimes reveals the meaning of aspects of Aelred's life by imposing a mathematical order upon them. This use of arithmetic and geometric relationships shows both the relative importance of related things and the progress of Aelred's growth in spiritual power. Writing of the effects of Aelred's abbacy at Rievaulx, for example, Walter contrasts the doubling of people and property with the trebling of 'the intensity of the monastic life and its charity' (38). When he tells of three prayers at three different stages of Aelred's monastic career, all for the same man's salvation and stability in monastic life, he shows them as all equally effective but each in succession more physically powerful. And by reporting two miraculous acts of healing done by Aelred at Revesby and four at Rievaulx he indicates the multiplication of Aelred's spiritual power over time.

However inadvertently, Walter also offers generous insights into his own personality in the course of the *Vita Aelredi*. From the prefatory letter on, Walter places himself at the center of the work, writing of his fears and feelings, his obligation to Abbot H, and his awareness of his own inadequacies. Indeed he seems hardly able to turn his attention to his subject, the memory of Aelred, because of obsession with himself:

> And yet, wretch that I am, what shall I do in the quandary in which I find myself? It strains my power and constrains my desire and blunts my will, for I long to do more than I can, and my will is to hold fast to the truth. (1)

Walter's inability to separate himself from his subject remains conspicuous throughout the work. Repeatedly he insists that it is he who decides what to include and in what detail:

> at this point I wish, with God's help, to describe (26),
> the same brother to whom I have referred above (30),

[8]Powicke, p. xv.

> I have seen him suspended in mid-air in a linen
>   sheet (39),
> What he touched his lips with I do not know, but I do
>   know that he at once broke out into speech (43),
> The father in that hour was sitting in the orchard . . . I
>   was there with him. (43)

Walter's apparent compulsion to call attention to his presence beside Aelred in the narrative of his life, all the while reporting his own thoughts and feelings, exposes his irritability and self-satisfaction, his firm opinions on topics ranging from rhetoric to ill health, his garrulousness and romanticism, his sensitivity to beauty, his devotion to cistercian life, and, above all, his love of Aelred. It is impossible to read the *Vita* without becoming well acquainted with Walter.

When Walter mentions Maurice, Aelred's predecessor in the abbacy, he not only reports that he had been 'called by his companions a second Bede', but adds his own judgment on the question: 'truly in his day, by his pre-eminence both in life and learning he alone could be compared with Bede. I myself have seen this man and knew him well, and I know how few men of his quality the world of mortal men contains' (33). And when he writes of Aelred's learning, he becomes so caught up in the topic that he forgets his subject (and seems entirely unaware of the personal implications of his digression):

> He never sought to involve his speech in the deceitful trappings which burden rather than enhance the value of its sense, because they rob truth of its meaning by digressions which it does not require and by additions which it disdains. For truth is self-contained; it needs no verbal artifice to explain and drive it home. Just as the sun, in order to shine, has no need for anything to make it shine more than it does shine, but would shine the less by any alien addition to it, so, to anyone who knows how to see it, the truth is sufficient in itself alone: if you impose something else upon it or mix something else with it, it becomes the less convincing just in so far as folly presumes to buttress up its inherent worth by what is foreign to it. . . . Verbiage can be meaningless, in no way different from the barking of a dog. (27)

Walter is not unaware of his tendency to hold forth, however, and from time to time he recalls himself from his extravagance with the words 'Well, as I have said' (12) or 'But enough of this' (27).

Walter's desire to be at the center of things and his pleasure at Aelred's friendship also appear throughout the *Vita* as he claims a special relationship with his abbot. When praising Aelred's writing he declares himself the preserver of the works 'by the labour of my own hand' (27), and when telling of Aelred's last days he makes a point of having been present and of Aelred's speaking to him from within his pain:

> then I came and saw the father sweating in anguish. . . . I said to a brother, 'Of a truth the lord abbot now suffers much. . . .' But he, gazing on me fondly—for he was so sweet—said, 'Yes, my son, yes, yes, just as you say; I am greatly vexed by the agonies of this sickness.' (56)

It may have been about 1155 that Walter became Aelred's scribe and thus his constant companion. All of Aelred's spiritual works except *The Mirror of Charity,* and several of his historical works, were probably written at or after that date, when Aelred was increasingly confined at home, turning his attention from the secular world to the need of monks and contemplatives for spiritual guidance. It is likely, then, that at this time he began to need a full-time secretary to assist with the increasing quantity of his work and, in his physically weakened state, perhaps to write at his dictation. Walter's responsibility for these tasks would inevitably give these years special importance in his account of Aelred's life.

Walter is especially pleased to be able to cite Aelred's own corroboration of their friendship in *Spiritual Friendship.* Where in his own narrative he can only assert his importance and hope to be believed, his representation as one of the participants in the dialogue of Aelred's work provides an enduring public acknowledgment of Aelred's affection for him. Walter is eager to ensure that no one miss the significance of that acknowledgment, reporting in his summary of *Spiritual Friendship* that Aelred 'joined me with himself in the . . . discussion' (41).

As Aelred's scribe, Walter must have been the person with whom Aelred most regularly talked during his final years. When he discussed his thoughts on spiritual friendship before writing them down, Walter—always at hand to care for him, to listen to him, to exchange authorial confidences and talk shop with him—must have been the one with whom he worked out his theological understanding. Aelred's representation of Walter in this capacity in *On Spiritual Friendship* preserves the memory not only of his place in Aelred's life during those years but of the affection Aelred had for this disciple, assistant, and intellectual companion.

But Walter's delight in being known as friend and assistant to Aelred has another, less pleasing aspect: an arrogance, a kind of self-centered resentment at opposition or challenge to himself or to Aelred. This aspect of his personality appears most notably in the Letter to Maurice, which he wrote in reply to critics of the *Vita*. To their charge that he had included miracles without proper substantiation and misrepresented Aelred's character, Walter retorts that they have not only failed to read his work closely but have shown an inadequate understanding of the conventions of rhetoric and a lack of familiarity with such cornerstones of the hagiographical tradition as Sulpicius Severus's *Life of Saint Martin.*

Such an attack on the literacy and intellectual abilities of his readers is surely consciously offensive. Walter is similarly rude in his response to their challenge to his description of the beauty of Aelred's body in death: 'You must pardon me, therefore, if I magnified the incomparable, as it deserved, by using a permissible hyperbole. If you do not, the experts in rhetoric will publicly trounce your stupidity' (77). While Walter's resentful assertion of his intellectual and moral superiority is especially common in the Letter, the tone here merely magnifies that in the *Vita*, where it is softened by the absence of cause for anger.

Walter's hostility toward attack, readiness to take offense, and defiant refusal to turn away wrath with a soft answer make him immediately recognizable in Aelred's portrait of him in *Spiritual Friendship*. He appears there as not only self-centered and garrulous but irascible and belligerent, complaining about the tardiness of the other participant in the dialogue and arguing that the spiritual friendship of which the abbot-teacher speaks is more than he aspires to and not really worth the trouble.

At one point Aelred places on the lips of the dialogue's abbot a pointed verbal caricature of Walter, portraying his irritation at being temporarily ignored:

A short while ago when I was carrying out worldly matters with men of the world, tell me why you sat alone a little removed from us? Now you kept shifting your gaze from this side to that, now you were rubbing your forehead with your hand, and again you were running your fingers through your hair. Again, with an angry frown or a frequent change of expression, you kept complaining that something contrary to your wishes had happened to you.[9]

Aelred's acerbic wit was never more evident.

In light of this portrait of irritability, the abbot's words later in the dialogue about the difficulties of friendship with an irascible man must be seen as a gentle chastisement of Walter:

Some are irascible by natural disposition. . . . At times . . . they offend a friend by a thoughtless act or remark or by indiscreet zeal. If perhaps we have welcomed such persons into friendship, we must suffer them with patience. Since we are assured of their affection, if there be any exaggeration in word or deed, we can excuse it in a friend or certainly point it out as an exaggeration, yet without bitterness and even lightheartedly.[10]

Walter's pleased boast that he is the Walter portrayed in this work indicates that he remained unchastened by these words and by the pointed nature of his representation. He must have been either so pleased to be noticed by Aelred and remembered in his writing that he ignored the significance of the passage or so lacking in self-criticism as to be deaf to its tone.

The bombastic nature of Walter's self-portrait in the *Vita* makes it difficult sometimes to understand the affection in which Aelred apparently held him. Insofar as Aelred was dependent on Walter's professional services as scribe and *medicus* he would often

[9]Spir amic 2.1; CCCM 1:302; CF 5:69: *nunc oculos huc illucque uertebas, nunc frontem confricabas manu, nunc capillos digitis attrectabas, nunc iram ipsa facie praeferens, aliquid tibi praeter uotum accessisse, crebra uultus mutatione querebaris, edicito.*
[10]Spir Amic 3.17; CCCM 1:320; CF 5:95.

have been unable to avoid Walter's presence, but it must have been by Aelred's own will that Walter obtained at least the first of these offices. Only affection can explain the warmth (combined with some exasperation) with which Aelred portrays Walter in *Spiritual Friendship* and the way in which he uses the portrait itself 'lightheartedly' to point out Walter's 'exaggeration', treating him precisely as the abbot in the work says a friend should be treated. One learns a great deal about Aelred's patience and Walter's own experience of it by recognizing what it must have required to tolerate years of close relationship with this warm-hearted but short-tempered man.

Aelred's fondness for his scribe may in part be explained by the appealing characteristics of Walter visible in the *Vita*: his love and veneration for Aelred, his appreciation for beauty, and his devotion to cistercian life. When he writes of Aelred's conversion he devotes an entire lengthy chapter to the excellence of life of the first community at Rievaulx and the beauty of the valley in which the abbey lies. By his description those first monks were angelic:

> wonderful men . . . white monks by name and white also in vesture. For their name arose from the fact that, as the angels might be, they were clothed in undyed wool spun and woven from the pure fleece of the sheep. . . . They venerate poverty . . . directed by a necessity of the will and sustained by the thoroughness of faith, and approved by divine love. They are welded together by such firm bands of charity that their society is as 'terrible as an army with banners.' (10-11)

And his sensuous words of pleasure in the valley's beauty explain part of the appeal that drew the Cistercians there and brought prosperity to the abbey:

> High hills surround the valley, encircling it like a crown. . . . From the loftiest rocks the waters wind and tumble down to the valley below, and as they make their hasty way through the lesser passages and narrower beds and spread themselves in wider rills, they give out a gentle murmur of soft sound and join together in the sweet notes of a delicious melody. (12-13)

Walter did not confine his romantic depiction of Rievaulx to the past, however, but wrote with similar enthusiasm of the monastery during his own experience of Aelred's abbacy, crediting its present success to Aelred's beneficent presence. In two chapters, one again lengthy, he writes of the Rievaulx he has known:

> It was the home of piety and peace, the abode of perfect love of God and neighbor. Who was there, however despised and rejected, who did not find in it a place of rest? Whoever came there in his weakness and did not find a loving father in Aelred and timely comforters in the brethren? . . . Hence it was that monks in need of mercy and compassion flocked to Rievaulx from foreign peoples and from the far ends of the earth, that there in very truth they might find peace and 'the holiness without which no man shall see God'. (36-37)

Walter's raptures, whether in paeans of celebratory praise or rages of defensive belligerence, contain much that is appealing. Despite his apparent inability to restrain his emotional response to the world, that response is not always angry, and his love for all that was good, along with his readiness to recognize and to respond to it with his whole heart, finally outweighs his irascibility for the modern reader as it must have for his abbot. Aelred could not have had a more devoted assistant.

Walter's character is of importance in any study of this, his most important work, because he and his viewpoint are inseparable from it. While not its subject and protagonist, he is its second most important character; the *Vita* becomes from time to time almost as much autobiography as biography: it is shaped by his presence and perspective. Thus Walter as well as Aelred survives through this work, not only as a reporter and interpreter but as the literary critic who evaluates his abbot's prose, the listener and medical adviser who stays at his side as he dies, and the mourner who washes his body and kisses his feet in death.

Walter's presentation of the *Vita* almost entirely through his own witness inevitably limits the work's scope. Aelred's life apart from what Walter knows either through observation or conversation with Aelred almost does not exist. Although Walter occasionally refers to another monk's confirmation of his stories, and in the Letter to Maurice indignantly names a multitude of other witnesses to the miracles, the largest part of what he recounts seems to have its source in his own experience, a fact which helps to explain the absence of information about Aelred's life outside the monastery.[11] The occasional exception, like the story of Aelred's intervention in the battles of Fergus of Galloway and his sons and his miracle of healing on the return to Rievaulx, suggests that Walter may have accompanied Aelred on that journey. Walter's horrified description of the beneficiary of Aelred's healing, a young man disfigured as a result of swallowing a tadpole that grew to maturity inside him, is unmistakeably a personal account (69).

Walter's ubiquitous presence in the *Vita* serves essentially to present the facts and, through them, the meaning of Aelred's life in such a way as to insist on their truth. The creator and narrator of the Life was also the witness of its substance, not as a recorder dependent on others' memories, but as someone personally present, personally accountable, and personally able to declare the truth of all he writes. Heffernan has noted Walter's insistence that 'the authentic "truth" of a situation is inextricably linked to a personal experience of it', that rather than the truth's existing independently of all observers, the observers are part of the reality.[12] Regarding the charges against the account of Aelred's life that prompted the Letter to Maurice, Heffernan notes:

> There is a striking contrast between, on the one hand, the skepticism of his critics who asked for facts somehow separable from the experience of those present and, on the other hand, Walter's ideas on the inseparability of the exact quality of the experience from the narratives of those who were there.[13]

The self-portrait of Walter Daniel in this work serves, then, not only to preserve information about his own life, experience, and character and to provide a window into the twelfth-century english cistercian understanding of monastic holiness, but to authenticate by his own witness the portrait of Aelred as one who embodied that understanding, as one who was a holy man, a

---

[11]I have discussed this point in more detail below in the section on the Sources of the *Vita*, pp. 46–49.
[12]Heffernan, p. 112.
[13]Heffernan, p. 110.

follower and imitator of Christ, an exemplar of God's presence in
the world.

Aelred was born in 1110 to the wife of Eilaf, the priest of
Saint Wilfrid's seventh-century church in the northumbrian city
of Hexham, not far from the border of Scotland. This Eilaf was
the son of another Eilaf, who had been treasurer of the cathedral
of Durham, and the grandson of Alfred son of Westou, sacristan of
the cathedral of Durham and guardian of the shrine there of Saint
Cuthbert. Alfred had first received the living at Hexham from
the bishop of Durham. He was, according to Aelred's *History of
the Saints of Hexham*, a learned man, known as Alfred *Larwa* or
'Teacher', and an enthusiastic collector of relics; he claimed to
have brought the bones of the Venerable Bede to Durham. The
younger Eilaf's three sons must have been expected to become in
their turn priests in the tradition of their fathers, probably at least
one in the church at Hexham.

But such a future was out of reach for Eilaf's sons. The
increasingly insistent attack of Gregorian Reform upon clerical
marriage in the twelfth century put an end to their hope of following their ancestors as secular priests.[15] Although the Church's
demand, first enunciated in 1074, that married priests put away
their wives and that unmarried priests remain so had been largely
ignored, by the early twelfth century newly powerful sanctions
were being imposed on married clergy and their families. As
priests refused to give up their wives and children, wives refused to leave their husbands, and lay people refused to reject

[14]The superb modern biography of Aelred, based on a study of the *Vita
Aelredi*, Aelred's own works, manuscript evidence, and other historical docu-
ments, is that of Aelred Squire, *Aelred of Rievaulx: A Study*, CS 50 (1969;
Kalamazoo: Cistercian, 1981).

[15]I have more fully discussed the impact of the movement toward cleri-
cal celibacy upon Aelred's life in 'The Conversion and Vocation of Aelred of
Rievaulx: A Historical Hypothesis', *England in the Twelfth Century*, ed. Daniel
Williams (London: Boydell, 1990) pp. 31–49 [henceforth Hypothesis].

the sacraments at the hands of married priests, Urban II ruled in 1095 that priests' sons could thenceforth not receive Holy Orders except as (safely celibate) canons regular or monks; in 1102 and again in 1108 Anselm, archbishop of Canterbury, reinforced Urban's decree, demanding anew that married clergy abandon their wives.[16]

Although the traditionally recalcitrant northerners were slow to accept the new strictures, by the time Aelred was born Eilaf's sons had been effectually barred from becoming secular priests. Aelred's brothers, Samuel and Aethelwold, apparently chose to be married laymen rather than cenobite priests, as the single historical reference to them, in Richard of Hexham's *History of the Church of Hexham,* identifies only Aelred as a monk.[17]

Eilaf's inability to look forward to his sons' succeeding him in the church at Hexham may help to explain the action in 1113 of Thomas II, archbishop of York, into whose gift the church at Hexham had come since the days of Alfred, when he transferred the spiritualities of Hexham to a community of augustinian canons, leaving the temporalities with Eilaf for his lifetime. The church was thus lost to the family that had cared for it for three generations, rebuilding it from ruin.

Aelred explains in *The Saints of Hexham* that it was Eilaf's initiative that had brought the canons:

> As this priest's devotion to the saints increased, he began to reflect more rigorously on his own unworthiness, on the sanctity of the church, and on reverence to the saints. Considering himself unworthy to approach such great fathers, he was also anxious lest the church be given to others no less worthy but certainly less careful after his death. Burning with zeal for the house of God, he went to that venerable man, the younger Thomas, archbishop of York, and humbly asked that he commit

---

[16]Johannes Dominicus Mansi, *Sacrorum conciliorum . . . collectio* (Florence, 1775) 20:724: Melfi, canon 14; 20:817: Clermont, canon 11. See also Anne L. Barstow, *Married Priests and the Reforming Papacy: The Eleventh-Century Debates* (New York: Mellen, 1982); and Christopher Brooke, 'Gregorian Reform in Action: Clerical Marriage in England, 1050–1200', *Cambridge Historical Journal* 12 (1956): 1–21.

[17]'Prior Richard's History of the Church of Hexham', ed. James Raine, *The Priory of Hexham*, vol. 1, Surtees Society 44 (Durham: Andrews, 1834) p. 55.

the church to the Canons Regular and hand over himself and his property to them.[18]

Recent discussions of this event have emphasized Eilaf's pain at seeing the canons take over the church, ignoring or explicitly rejecting Aelred's explanation. Powicke, for example, interprets Walter's remark in the Letter to Maurice that Eilaf 'felt very sore'[19] as an allusion to Eilaf's hostility toward Thomas for sending canons to Hexham. But the passage in question, in which the young Aelred tells his father of the archbishop's death and his father responds with a reference to Thomas's 'evil life' (72), provides tenuous grounds in the absence of any corroborating evidence of a tradition of hostility between Eilaf's family and the canons.

Prior Richard's *History of the Church of Hexham* provides additional insight, though not much clarity. Richard recalls that during the days when the canons were first at Hexham, Eilaf held 'the greater part of the property of the church' along with parcels of land in both Hexham and the nearby village of Aynewyk while the canons endured poverty and hunger. But, he goes on to say, in time Eilaf 'repented for having so long detained the things of the church, by which the servants of God ought rightly to have been sustained', and in 1138, shortly before becoming a monk at Durham, he donated his remaining property to the canons.[20]

These conflicting perspectives on the coming of the canons to Hexham suggest that the growing effectiveness of papal reform may have led Eilaf to decide, however unwillingly, to free himself from the responsibilities of his church. Once he became aware that despite his and his father's struggles at Hexham the property would soon pass from the family, perhaps he found the work required by the fragile old church no longer worth the effort. His arrangement with the canons may then have come about as part of a negotiation between Eilaf and Thomas for the future of Eilaf's intelligent

[18]'On the Saints of Hexham', ed. James Raine, *The Priory of Hexham*, vol. 1, Surtees Society 44 (Durham: Andrews, 1834) p. 192 [henceforth Raine]; 'The Saints of Hexham', trans. Jane Patricia Freeland, *The Historical Works of Aelred of Rievaulx*, CF 56 (Kalamazoo: Cistercian—forthcoming).
[19]Powicke, pp. xxxv and 72n.
[20]Raine, pp. 55–6.

young son.[21] Such an explanation would reconcile Aelred's claim that the coming of the canons was his father's idea with the implication of Prior Richard's account that Eilaf yielded no more of the Hexham property than he had to. The net effect, however, was that Aelred would never be priest at Hexham, would never follow his great-grandfather, grandfather, and father in serving at the altar of Saint Andrew's,[22] and could never hope for holy Orders except within conventual life.

Aelred's intelligence must have been apparent from his earliest years. Walter, writing about him many years later, notes that 'he had been given, as he retained, natural capacity to a high degree' (26) and comments that 'he had at his command all the resources of splendid eloquence and a noble flow of words' (27). Similarly Gilbert of Hoyland records in his eulogy for Aelred that he was 'acutely intelligent'.[23] Stories of Aelred's childhood in the Letter to Maurice also suggest that he was regarded from infancy as an uncommonly bright lad. No one who reads Aelred's works can doubt that he was both intellectually gifted and spiritually graced; his parents surely gave serious thought to the life choices available to their son. Whether because of arrangements made through the archbishop of York or otherwise, somehow Aelred received an education and career training highly unusual for the child of a parish priest.

---

[21]See my discussion of Aelred's conversion in Hypothesis, pp. 38–9. I am grateful to W. F. McCulloch for the suggestion that Eilaf may have offered Thomas the Hexham church in exchange for his making provision for Aelred's future.

[22]A poignant memorial of that historical reality hangs on the wall of Saint Andrew's Church in Hexham, where a plaque naming the saints, priests, and priors of Hexham lists only three priests: Alfred, Eilaf, and Eilaf. Aelred's name is absent, and he himself until a few years ago was not remembered as a son of the parish.

[23]S. 40 [PL 41.6]; PL 184:216; CF 26:496. Since the fifteenth century the editorial tradition of Gilbert's sermons has incorrectly numbered the second portion of sermon 11 as sermon 12 and the subsequent sermons as 13 through 48 rather than 12 through 47. Sermon 40 is therefore number 41 in both the PL edition and the CF translation. The number is, however, correct in the french translation of Pierre-Yves Emery, *Sermons sur le* Cantique des Cantiques, Pain de Cîteaux 6 (Oka: Notre-Dame-du Lac, 1994); see p. 157. My forthcoming edition of Gilbert's works in Corpus Christianorum, Continuatio Mediaevalis will also number the sermons in accord with the manuscript tradition.

Aelred apparently received a few years of education in the cathedral school at Durham, to which his family retained close ties. Laurence, a friend of Eilaf and a monk of Durham who was apparently one of his masters there, later dedicated to Aelred his Life of Saint Brigit, prefacing it with a letter commending his former student's continuing interest in learning and literature.[24] But after a few years at Durham, in about 1124, Aelred entered the court of David I of Scotland, where he remained for ten years. Walter Daniel says of his education that he 'acquired but little knowledge in the world', adding that he

> felt rather than absorbed what the authorities call the liberal arts, by the process of oral instruction in which the master's voice enters the pupil's breast; but in all other respects he was his own master, with an understanding far beyond that of those who have learned the elements of secular knowledge from the injection of words rather than from the infusion of the Holy Spirit. (26)

Jocelin of Furness writes of Aelred in *The Life of Saint Waldef*: 'His school learning was slight, but as a result of careful self-discipline in the exercise of his acute natural powers, he was cultured above many who have been thoroughly trained in secular learning.'[25]

Although nothing of Aelred's secular learning is known apart from these comments, his youthful acquaintance with classical learning is evident in his adaptation of Cicero's *De amicitia* in his *Spiritual Friendship* and in the evidence that work gives of his profound familiarity with Cicero's work. Again, his reference in *The Mirror of Charity* to 'tragedies or epic poetry' and to 'fables . . . in common speech about some Arthur' shows his familiarity with literature both classical and contemporary.[26]

Aelred received further education and career training in David's court at Roxborough. Growing up with David's son and stepsons, he must have been educated with them, although whereas

[24]Anselm Hoste, OSB, 'A Survey of the Unedited Works of Laurence of Durham', *Sacris Erudiri* 11 (1960) 248–65.

[25]Jocelin of Furness, *Vita S. Waldeni, Acta Sanctorum*, August, 1: 257d; quoted from Powicke, p. xxxiii.

[26]Spec car 2.17.50–51; CCCM 1:90; CF 17:198–9. I am grateful to Elizabeth Connor, OCSO, for bringing this passage to my attention.

David's son and older stepson could look forward to inheriting wealth and power, Aelred could expect always to be in an inferior position as an educated clerk or steward to his lord. As Aelred matured, in fact, he became David's *echonomus* or steward, serving at court and on diplomatic missions around Scotland and in the North of England and thereby meeting such great figures of David's reign as Walter Espec, one of the 'new men' of Henry I of England and the future founder of Rievaulx.

About Aelred's personal life and relationships at David's court almost nothing is known. Walter's only indication in the *Vita* of the presence of other inhabitants of the household or of Aelred's interaction with them appears in the story of a knight (described by Walter, predictably, as 'a certain hard, stiff dolt of a fellow, quite intractable . . . and certainly strong and cruel enough in evil') whose jealousy provoked him first to try 'to excite feelings of indignation against [Aelred] among his fellow-warriors' (5) and finally to burst out in a public attack on Aelred's unworthiness 'to have the disposal of the King's treasure and to be in his personal service and enjoy such praise and distinction' (6). This man, Walter says, was won over to friendship with Aelred by the patience with which Aelred admitted his own inadequacy to serve David 'as he should be served' and his confession that 'I am a sinner, and have failed much in my service, not to the king whom I serve on earth, but to the King of heaven' (7).

Although Walter says that in time the angry knight became attached in friendship to Aelred, his closer friends seem, on the basis of external evidence and of passages in his own works, to have been the stepson and son of the king. His friendship in later years with Waldef, the second son of Matilda of Saint Liz of Huntingdon and stepson of David, was surely a continuation from their youth: Jocelin of Furness attributes to Aelred's influence Waldef's leaving the Austin canons at Kirkham to become a Cistercian and reports later visits between Aelred and Waldef when Waldef was abbot of Rievaulx's daughter-house at Melrose.[27]

[27]Jocelin of Furness, pp. 257, 264–66; Powicke, p. lxxv.

In *The Genealogy of the Kings of England* Aelred recalls his youthful friendship with Prince Henry: 'I lived with [Henry] from the very cradle, and we grew up as children together. When I was a boy I knew him as a boy, when he was stamping out the flowers of youth like his father, whom I loved beyond all mortals.'[28] His praise for the prince's virtue and courage in *Battle of the Standard* is surely rooted in their youth together:

> He was a young man fair of face and handsome in appearance, so humble that he seemed lower than everyone, of such authority that he was held in awe by everyone, and so gentle, pleasant, and agreeable that he was loved by everyone. He was so chaste in body, so sober in his speech, so honorable in all his ways, so diligent in church and attentive in prayer, so kind to the poor and so resolute against malefactors, and so respectful toward priests and monks, that he seemed to be a monk in a king and a king in a monk.[29]

While it is difficult to draw certain conclusions about Aelred's youthful friendships from his works, his insistence on the moral and spiritual value of friendship between members of the same sex and of opposite sexes, even when it is inevitably broken by separation and death, indicates the value he placed on such relationships. His apparent recollection in *The Mirror of Charity* of one youthful friendship thus helps to complete the picture of his life, despite its failure to identify the friend, the gender of the friend, or the nature of the friendship:

> the fetters of gracious company pressed upon me tightly; above all the knot of a certain friendship was dearer to me than all the delights of my life. . . . I recognized that sweetness was mixed with bitterness, sadness with joy, adversity with prosperity. The charming bond of friendship gratified me.[30]

The only real insight Walter gives into Aelred's personal relationships while at court appears in the Letter to Maurice. There he casually admits Aelred's youthful sexual activity in explanation of a charge leveled against the *Vita*: 'It is that, because in that

[28]Gen; PL 195:736–37; CF 56.
[29]Bello; PL 195:708; CF 56.
[30]Spec car 1.28.79; CCCM 1:47; CF 17:134.

same period of his life Aelred occasionally deflowered his chastity I ought not to have compared a man of that sort to a monk' (76). But the topic was of such little interest to Walter that it is impossible to infer either the gender or the number of Aelred's sexual partners, the nature or endurance of any sexual relationship he may have had, or his own attitude toward his sexual experience. While Aelred's own written references to sex provide more opportunities for guesswork on the subject, they give no more knowledge. In *On the Institution of Recluses,* for example, he writes of his loss of chastity, adding that 'I freely abandoned myself to all that is base, accumulating material for fire to burn me, for corruption to stifle me, for worms to gnaw me.'[31] But as this passage is highly dependent on Augustine's description of himself in *The Confessions,*[32] it adds no more clarity than circumstance to the history of Aelred's sexual experience.[33]

In 1134, putting the youthful pleasures of the court behind him, Aelred became a monk at the new cistercian house in York-shire, the first one founded in the North of England. Walter explains that while on a journey to York Aelred serendipitously learned of the new monastery of white monks. After a day's visit there and a night's thought about what he had seen, Walter says, he returned the next day as a postulant for admission and was welcomed on his arrival by the entire community.

It seems likely, despite Walter's version of the story, that Aelred travelled to England in part to visit the new community, whose abbot was William, formerly the secretary of the renowned Bernard of Clairvaux, and whose founding figures were Arch-bishop Thurstan of York and Walter Espec, both of whom he had surely known for many years. David of Scotland seems also to have played a role in the establishment of Rievaulx, as a letter from

[31]Inst incl 32; CCCM 1:674; CF 2:93–4.
[32]Conf 2.7; CCCL 27:24–5; *Confessions,* trans. R. S. Pine-Coffin (Har-mondsworth: Penguin, 1961) p. 51.
[33]I have presented all the passages from Aelred's treatises discussing friend-ship, marriage, chastity, and sex, arguing for the impossibility of using such pas-sages to determine anything about his sexual experience, in 'Aelred of Rievaulx on Friendship, Chastity, and Sex: The Sources', CSQ 29 (1994).

Bernard in 1134, asking for his support for the new foundation at Fountains, recalls: 'The brethren at Rievaulx first knew the effects of your mercy. You opened to them the treasury of your good will and anointed them with the oil of your compassion and kindness.'[34] Whatever the influences that led Aelred to the new abbey of white monks, whether his decision was long-pondered or pauline in its suddenness, his turning on that day from the world to the cloister was a true conversion, redolent of spiritual power and enduring significance. Walter's statement that Aelred could, had he wished, have become bishop of Saint Andrew's (3) is probably untrue: as the son of a priest he could not have been admitted to holy orders outside of cenobitic life. But Walter is correct in insisting on the significance of Aelred's choice of a life devoted to the *via contemplativa* rather than the *via activa,* a life to be spent within a community ruled by the *Regula Benedicti* and enclosed, at least symbolically, by the cloister wall. Aelred's entry into monastic life on that day in 1134 was the defining act of his life.

Although Bernard later recalled Aelred's having described himself as one who had come from the kitchen to the desert,[35] the kitchen was as much a metaphor as was the desert. Aelred came not from pots, pans, blancmange, and tansy cakes to silence and solitude in the Rye valley, but from 'the counsels of an earthly king' to an apprenticeship in administration and diplomacy under the abbot of Rievaulx (8). Whatever Aelred gave up to become a monk, he never forgot what he had learned in and about the world. The reputation his diplomatic abilities gained for Rievaulx as he acted in affairs of Church and crown over the next thirty years contributed to the renown and prosperity not only of that house but of the Cistercian Order in England.

The years of responsibility at David's court had served Aelred well. It quickly became apparent, if it had not been before he

[34]SBOp 8:478.
[35]SBOp 8:486–89. Bernard's letter, in which he directs Aelred to write the work that he called *Speculum caritatis,* is translated at the beginning of the new translation of that work, *The Mirror of Charity,* trans. Elizabeth Connor, ocso, CF 17 (Kalamazoo: Cistercian, 1990) p. 69.

entered, that Rievaulx would benefit from his experience as steward and diplomat. As his obedience in service to David had readied him for a new life of discipline and humility before his monastic superiors, so his familiarity with the court and with those who lived or visited there had made him comfortable with those in high places and easy in the exercise of authority and diplomacy. Abbot William quickly recognized his skills and made good use of them.

Aelred's public life began early. In 1138, as the civil war between Stephen and Matilda for the english throne moved northward, Aelred probably accompanied his abbot to the scottish border to negotiate Walter Espec's surrender of his castle at Wark to King David.[36] That same year Aelred and William were in Hexham for Eilaf's donation of his remaining property to the canons.[37] And in 1142 Aelred represented William in a party of northern prelates journeying to Rome to protest before Innocent II the naming of another William, the nephew of King Stephen of England, as Archbishop of York.[38]

At the same time that Aelred was distinguishing himself outside the monastery and displaying the skills that were to be of public value in the years to come he was also taking on increasing responsibility at home. Upon his return from Rome he became novice master at Rievaulx, then in 1143 helped to establish Rievaulx's third daughter house, Saint Laurence of Revesby, which he served as abbot until 1147.

The years at Revesby seem to have been of mixed success for the young abbot. While Walter celebrates the increase of Aelred's fame and popularity in the neighborhood and his success at obtaining land for the monastery, he also seems anxious to justify the methods:

[36]Raine, p. 100; 'The Chronicle of John, Prior of Hexham', ed. Raine, p. 118; see also Powicke, p. xlvi.

[37]Raine, p. 55.

[38]Squire, pp. 23–4; C. H. Talbot, 'New Documents in the Case of St William of York', *Cambridge Historical Journal* 10 (1950): 1–15; David Knowles, 'The Case of St William of York', reprinted in *The Historian and Character* (Cambridge, 1963) pp. 76–97.

Bishop, earls, barons venerate the man and the place itself, and in their reverence and affection load it with possessions, heap gifts upon it and defend it by their peace and protection. The bishop orders him to preach to the clergy in their local synods, and he does so; to bring priests to a better way of life, as he does not fail to do; to accept grants of land from knights in generous free-alms, and he obeys, since he had realized that in this unsettled time such gifts profited knights and monks alike, for in those days it was hard for any to lead the good life unless they were monks or members of some religious order. . . . and he knew that to give what they had helped the possessors of goods to their salvation, and that, if they did not give, they might well lose both life and goods without any payment in return. (28)

Walter's haste to explain that the benefit of these gifts was as great for the donors as for the recipients suggests that Aelred's enthusiasm in soliciting donations of property from his new neighbors had brought with it some criticism. Such defensiveness indicates both Walter's belief that it was necessary to refute the charge and his continual concern to defend his abbot even while eulogizing him. But he provides an intriguing insight into the conflicts and sometimes troubled public reputation of the energetic young abbot of Revesby.

The story is a familiar one. As the Bible reports that God chose Jacob, a man of craft, guile, luck, and economic foresight, to found and father Israel, so in twelfth-century Lincolnshire Aelred, educated and experienced in the exercise of power and in developing working relationships with local magnates, proved himself an able man of business, a founder and abbot *par excellence*, successfully carrying out the task he had been given by hobnobbing with his neighbors, enlisting the rich and powerful in his efforts to build the new community.

While Aelred's primary goal at Revesby was probably to secure economic self-sufficiency for the new community, a concern of any founder, he was at the same time responsible for establishing a regular life of prayer and contemplation there. Walter reports that he was successful on both counts:

> Within, the religious life waxed every hour and grew day by
> day; without, possessions increased and gave a regular return in
> money and means for all kinds of equipment. . . . There was
> no sterility there, for our Jacob begat twins by both Leah and
> Rachel, as he preached fear and justice to the administrative
> staff and impressed the duties of prayer and love upon the
> contemplatives in the cloister. (29)

The success Aelred experienced at Revesby as a forceful property manager is generally overlooked by those who remember him
today as primarily a gentle spiritual writer. Walter's emphasis in
the *Vita* on Aelred's last years of frailty and pain has tended to
obscure the energetic young abbot who quickly turned the new
foundation at Revesby into a going concern.

But the former novice master, whose spiritual power and gifts
for teaching monks the love of God had impressed Bernard of
Clairvaux, had not vanished in the new role at Revesby. Abbot
William must have chosen Aelred to lead the new abbey precisely
because he was uniquely able to create a life of the spirit while
at the same time erecting an enduring community. As surely as
his training under David had prepared him for subsequent public
roles, this first abbacy prepared him for the one that would be his
life's work.

In 1147 Aelred was elected abbot of his home community.
It seems likely that he had been in line for this position since
early in his monastic career; his positions as first novice master
and then abbot of Revesby were probably intended to give him
the experience necessary for governing this large and important
abbey. Even so, his election seems not to have been assured, but to
have occasioned conflict within the community. After reporting
that upon the resignation of Abbot Maurice 'Aelred was duly
chosen by the brethren in his place', Walter comments that 'There
are some who think that ambition brought him to the headship
of this house' (33) and at once denies the truth of the charge:
'Every good man knows that this is false'. While he attributes it
to jealousy of Aelred's virtue, Walter's characteristically pugnacious
denial preserves the memory of dissent in the community and of
some personal resentment of the new abbot.

The difficulty and opposition experienced by Aelred in the early years of his abbacy gains additional significance from Walter Daniel's report of both the election and rumors about Aelred in the same chapter. Immediately after rejecting the accusation that Aelred was ambitious, Walter explains other but related rumors: 'Some said that he was a good man, others, "No, he is a glutton and a wine-bibber and a friend of publicans, and gives up his body to baths and ointments" ' (34). These complaints must have been connected to objections to Aelred as abbatial candidate: not only did he seek election, his opponents said, but he was a bad monk, self-indulgent, still accustomed to the sensuous luxuries of his life in court fourteen years earlier and still too involved in the world.

Despite the personal conflicts Aelred apparently encountered upon becoming abbot at Rievaulx, he was, according to Walter, as effective there as he had been at Revesby, again strengthening the community in both size and virtue. As at Revesby he had created a new monastery strong in both religious life and economic well-being, so during his years at Rievaulx he brought both economic and spiritual growth to an already large and successful abbey: 'He doubled all things in it—monks, *conversi*, laymen, farms, lands and every kind of equipment; indeed he trebled the intensity of the monastic life and its charity' (38).

Walter's emphasis is clear and intentional. Aelred was in both of his abbacies a successful manager, able to increase the property value of the monasteries he governed. He was even more successful, Walter says, as a spiritual father, a shaper of monks who loved God, one another, and the weak and poor beyond their gates. Further, it was through this increase of charity that the monasteries grew and prospered.

At the same time that Aelred was building up his two monasteries, he was also building a reputation in the world beyond the cloister. Although some hint of the range of his activities in the kingdom and in the english church can be drawn from the *Vita,* he was clearly much more popular as a guest preacher and political counselor than Walter ever suggests. Some of his own works indicate that he was invited to preach at the translation of

the saints of Hexham in 1155, at an event of similar importance at
Whithorn in Galloway sometime between 1147 and 1166, and at
the translation of Edward the Confessor at Westminster in 1163;
according to Reginald of Durham he also preached at the church
in Kircudbright on Saint Cuthbert's day 1164.[39]

Of those events and the many others they represent Walter
mentions only that he 'preached about two hundred most eloquent
sermons . . . in our chapters, in synods and to the people' (42)
and that 'he expounded [*exposuit*] in honour of [Edward the
Confessor] and to be read with the passage at his solemn vigils the
gospel lesson' (41). He leaves unanswered the question of Aelred's
presence at those vigils or the translation, at which he might be
expected to have presented the *Life of Saint Edward,* written at the
request of the abbot of Westminster.[40]

In addition to preaching on great occasions, Aelred traveled
frequently around Scotland and England, witnessing his father's
donation to the canons at Hexham, negotiating peace between
Fergus of Galloway and his sons, advising monastic communities
in cases of conflict like the one discussed in *The Nun of Watton,* and
visiting friends such as Waldef of Melrose and Godric of Finchale.
Walter Daniel reports that the successful outcome of Aelred's
negotiations with Fergus and his sons led Fergus to enter monastic
life (46); though he does not name the monastery, Fergus died a
monk of the cistercian abbey of Holyrood. Reginald of Durham,
who wrote the life of Godric, credits Aelred with persuading him
to investigate and write the Life of the former pirate and holy
hermit: 'I have been at length not so much asked as compelled to
write by many friends most dear to me, and especially by Dom

[39]Reginald of Durham, *De admirandis Beati Cuthberti uirtutibus*, Surtees Society 8 (London: Nichols, 1835) pp. 178–9; see also p. 9.

[40]Two contemporary documents record Aelred's presence at the translation:
Chronicon Angliae Petriburgense, ed. J. A. Giles (1845; New York: Franklin, 1967)
p. 98, AD 1163; and Richard of Cirencester, *De gestis regum Angliae*, ed. J. E.
B. Mayor, vol. 2 (London: Longmans, 1869) p. 326. Aelred is portrayed in a
fourteenth-century manuscript of the *Vita S. Edwardi* (Dublin MS TCD 172)
presenting the work to Henry II in the presence of Laurence of Westminster,
who commissioned it; this image represents the translation of 13 October 1163,
and indicates the illustrator's expectation that Aelred would have been present.

Aelred, abbot of Rievaulx; and what I did not already know, the more carefully to inquire into.'[41] Aelred's influence went beyond the world of the Church, bridging the gap between Church and crown. *The Peterborough Chronicle* for 1162 credits Aelred with bringing about Henry II's decisive support for Pope Alexander III.[42] This assertion, although representing a fourteenth-century memory, is supported by the issuance of a bull of protection and confirmation from Alexander to Rievaulx, addressed to Aelred and the monks on 21 December 1160, soon after Henry's decision for Alexander became publicly known.[43]

Alexander's canonization of Edward the Confessor, the last anglo-saxon king of England, in prompt reciprocation for Henry's support, also brought Aelred the opportunity to write the Confessor's Life. This work, which explicitly defined the Normans and Plantagenets as rightful heirs to the anglo-saxon monarchy, established the political legitimacy of Henry and his successors.[44] While Laurence of Westminster asked Aelred to write the Life of Edward, as Walter records in the *Vita* (41–42) and Aelred in the prefatory letter to the *Life of Saint Edward*, Henry II may well have had a voice in his selection, as the abbot of Rievaulx was apparently already known to him as a trusted adviser.

The documentary evidence of Henry's acquaintance with Aelred and, hence, of Aelred's influence on him is slight, but it reaches from before Henry became king to a few years before Aelred's death. In 1154, just after Henry was named King

---

[41] 19: *A pluribus tandem amicis mihi carissimis, et quam maxime a domno Edeldredo Rievallensi abate, non tam rogatus quam compulsus sum ea quae audieram scribere; et quae nec dum noveram, sollicitius investigare.* See also pp. 173, 176–7.

[42] *Chronicon Angliae Petriburgense*, p. 96: *Rex Henricus honorifice recepit papam Alexandrum versus Gallias venientem, inductus ad ejus obedientiam per literas Arnulfi episcopi Luxoviensis, et maxime viva voce sancti Alredi abbatis Rievallensis.*

[43] J. C. Atkinson, ed., *Cartularium Abbathiae de Rievalle*, Surtees Society 83 (Durham: Andrews, 1889) pp. 185–8.

[44] I have discussed Aelred's role in the election of Alexander and his creation of the Plantagenet myth in *The Life of Saint Edward, King and Confessor*: 'Aelred historien: deux nouveaux portraits dans un manuscrit de Dublin', *Collectanea Cisterciensia* 53 (1993): 208–30; and 'Aelred, Historian: Two Portraits in Plantagenet Myth', *CSQ* 28 (1993): 112–44 [henceforth *Portraits*].

Stephen's heir, Aelred addressed his *Genealogy of the Kings of England* to him, urging this descendent of anglo-saxon and norman kings to live in virtuous and faithful imitation of his great predecessors on the throne of England. And on 8 March 1163, Aelred was one of twenty-five witnesses—with Thomas Becket, archbishop of Canterbury, and Laurence, abbot of Westminster—to Henry's confirmation of an agreement on episcopal rights between the bishop of Lincoln and the abbot of Saint Alban's.[45]

Aelred's acquaintance with Henry may have begun before or during the english Civil War while the young Duke of Normandy and Count of Anjou fought on behalf of his mother Matilda for the crown, as David of Scotland was Henry's uncle and patron. Walter suggests that Aelred may also have been known to King Stephen, who reigned from 1135 to 1154. During those years Stephen was the enemy of both David and Henry, but was overlord to Walter Espec, patron and founder of Rievaulx. Writing of Aelred as abbot of Revesby from 1143 to 1147, Walter states that he was 'greatly beloved by all in the province, indeed by the whole realm and most of all by the king' (29).

Walter is probably in error here, either thinking of Aelred's friendship in his own time with Henry II and forgetting that while Aelred was at Revesby Stephen was king or misunderstanding Aelred's reminiscences about his royal connections. If he is correct, however, Aelred's political acumen and influence with the great figures of England were even greater than has been previously recognized, and the careful neutrality of his narrative of the 1138 Battle of the Standard between the armies of Stephen and David is the more comprehensible.

Aelred was apparently well known to the great figures of the twelfth-century world. Many would have been already known to him from his days at David's court, and his 1142 trip to Rome in company with the prelates of the North would have increased and strengthened his connections. Once he was abbot

[45] *The Registrum antiquissimum of the Cathedral Church of Lincoln*, ed. C. W. Foster, Lincoln Record Society 27, vol. 1 (Hereford: The Lincoln Record Society, 1931) pp. 65–6, no. 104.

of Revesby, moreover, he had even more pressing reason to meet the regional magnates. Like other monastic figures of his time, such as Hildegard of Bingen and Bernard of Clairvaux, he maintained his relationships with these people, whom he met as part of the ordinary business of his life, by means of an active correspondence which Walter says Aelred began while novice master. And toward the end of his life, Walter reports:

> he was sending letters to the lord pope, to the king of France, the king of England, the king of Scotland, the archbishops of Canterbury and York and nearly every bishop in England, also to the most distinguished men in the kingdom of England and especially to the Earl of Leicester, letters written with a noble pen to every grade of the ecclesiastical order, in which he left a living image of himself. (42)

Whether Aelred was able to exercise active influence on those figures, such widespread correspondence indicates at least his having had the opportunity to consult with and advise them. His letters, listed in the thirteenth-century catalogue of Rievaulx, still existed in the fifteenth century, when an extract from one of them was copied into the manuscript of the catalogue, but have since then vanished.[46]

Aelred's involvement in the world outside Rievaulx must have kept him often—perhaps too often—away from his responsibilities at home. His own concern about these frequent journeys and the demands made on him and the community by his relationship with Henry II appears in Walter's report of his final address to the monks, given nine days before his death:

> Often I have begged your permission when I had to cross the sea, or it was my duty to hasten to some distant region, or I had occasion to seek the king's court; and now by your leave and with the help of your prayers I go hence, from exile to fatherland, from darkness to light, from this evil world to God. (57)

---

[46]Anselm Hoste, *Bibliotheca Aelrediana*, Instrumenta Patristica 2 (The Hague: Nijhoff, 1962) pp. 147–76; M. R. James, *A Descriptive Catalogue of the Manuscripts in the Library of Jesus College, Cambridge*, p. 44; Powicke, p. c.

At the end of his life Aelred recalls the two poles between which his life has moved and associates them with the tension between the earthly kingdom and the heavenly.[47] In Aelred's last years, despite occasional trips outside Rievaulx, like that to Westminster in 1163, he was increasingly weak and troubled by pain. Like Bernard before him, he was allowed by the General Chapter in 1157 to live in and conduct his business from the monastic infirmary. Soon he moved into a small hut built on the grounds near the infirmary—Walter calls it variously a *mausoleum* (39), a *tugurium* (40), and a *secretario* (41)—there to read, write, sleep, eat, and receive visitors.

Aelred's illness seems to have been a combination of kidney stone, arthritis, and perhaps shingles, according to details Walter gives. Despite his excruciating pain as 'he sacrificed himself on the altar of unfailing suffering' (49), his sickroom became a gathering place for the monks, who sat and talked both among themselves and with him. As he approached his end, Walter says, 'There were now twelve, now twenty, now forty, now even a hundred monks about him; so vehemently was this lover of us all loved by us' (59). At last he was theirs, able to give them the time and attention and spiritual guidance that over the years had so often gone to other communities and to public figures.

That was also the period of Aelred's life most available to Walter's observation and hence to the *Vita*. Walter's close acquaintance with his abbot surely developed in part because Aelred had an increasing need of the medical attention that Walter seems to have been ready to give, in part because Aelred had perhaps pressed his educated *medicus* into service as secretary and scribe.

The ailments that kept Aelred at home and afforded opportunity for members of the community to receive regular spiritual counsel from him also provided material for Walter's depiction of him as a gentle, loving, holy man who offered spiritual guidance through both conversation and the treatises he wrote for a wider

---

[47]These words may of course be Walter's rather than Aelred's, but their bearing on the historical detail of Aelred's life is the same. See Heffernan, pp. 77–80.

audience. The picture of him and of his relationships with the community that appears in the *Vita* is thus probably radically different from what it would have been had Walter worked beside him and written of him earlier in his career.

The difference in Aelred himself and the life at Rievaulx between the early years of his abbacy and the late years, when he had ample time for his monks, is borne out by his fictional depiction of himself as abbot in relationship to his monks in *Spiritual Friendship*. He wrote this work sometime after 1164, perhaps looking back with a certain regret at his years of activity, regret for their loss and perhaps also nostalgia at the memory of conversations interrupted and friendships not adequately cherished. In that work he describes the community and his love for its members as an anticipation of beatitude:

> The day before yesterday, as I was walking the round of the cloister of the monastery, the brethren were sitting around forming as it were a most loving crown. In the midst, as it were, of the delights of paradise with the leaves, flowers, and fruits of each single tree, I marveled. In that multitude of brethren I found no one whom I did not love, and no one by whom, I felt sure, I was not loved. I was filled with such joy that it surpassed all the delights of this world.[48]

Aelred's awareness of and frustration at the inability of an abbot to spend time in loving conversation with his monks because of his official duties and official guests whom he described as 'hustling me off to other business'[49] appear clearly in this late work, concretely exemplifying the work's theme: the inevitability of interruptions—both transitory and permanent—in human relationships and the promise of their restoration and permanence with God in beatitude.

However often Aelred left home for court during his years as abbot, it was the community at Rievaulx that claimed his heart and gave him his warmest memories. As he prepared to leave his earthly home and those who had shared it with him, Walter

---

[48]Spir amic 3.82; CCCM 1:334; CF 5:112.
[49]Spir amic 2.71; CCCM 1:315; CF 5:87: *importunitate compellunt.*

reports, Aelred spoke of the life of Rievaulx and of his spiritual sons whom he had brought to life and nourished there:

> For the time has come when he, who . . . deigned by his grace to bind me more closely to himself in the bonds of a better life among you, will take me to himself. . . . God who knows all things knows that I love you all as myself, and, as earnestly as a mother after her sons, 'I long after you all in the bowels of Jesus Christ'. (57-58)

As Christmas 1166 approached, Aelred had become so weak that he was unable even to drag himself to community Mass. Lying near unconsciousness he cried out in his longing for death, now uniting the language of his adult years with that of his childhood, the Latin of the monastery with the English of his ancestors: '*Festinate, for crist luve*', 'Hasten, for the love of Christ' (60).

Death came at last during the night of 12 January 1167.[50] On the day before Aelred died, Walter says, two other cistercian abbots, Richard of Fountains and Roger of Byland, 'with nearly all the monks and several of the *conversi*', stood around his bed. As one monk read the story of Christ's Passion aloud, Walter held Aelred's head in his hands that he might gaze upon the crucifix. So supported, Aelred spoke the last words Walter attributes to him, the words of the Psalmist spoken by Christ on the cross: 'Thou art my God and my Lord, Thou art my refuge and my Saviour. Thou art my glory and my hope for evermore. Into Thy hands I commend my spirit' (61).[51]

As death approached the monks placed Aelred on a hair-cloth strewn with ashes, 'as monastic custom is'; there he died, in the presence of four abbots and 'the brethren'. His body washed, Roger of Byland anointed it with 'a little of the balsam which the father had had as medicine'. At last, his long suffering past, his

---

[50]Walter reports that Aelred died at 'about the fourth watch of the night before the Ides of January', which is to say at about 10:30. Although Walter gives the year as 1166, he would have been following the old style calendar, according to which the year changed on March 25; by the current calendar Aelred died in 1167.

[51]Luke 23:46; cf. Psalm 30 [AV 31]. Much of Heffernan's discussion of the *Vita Aelredi* focuses on the significance of these words in Walter's treatment of Aelred; see pp. 74–87.

body was taken to the church for Mass and funeral rites, then to the chapter house for burial next to Abbot William, in company with whom, Walter concludes, 'he will rejoice and be glad exceedingly, as is right, before God and Our Lord Jesus Christ, to whom be the glory for ever and ever. Amen' (62-4).

Aelred's death at once brought words of grief from friends outside Rievaulx. Gilbert of Hoyland, abbot of the Lincolnshire abbey of Swineshead, incorporated a eulogy for Aelred into Sermon 40 of his sermons on the Song of Songs, praising

> his modest countenance and the tranquil bearing of his whole body . . . the calm affections of his spirit. He was lucid in interpretation, not hasty in speech. He questioned modestly, replied more modestly, tolerating the troublesome, himself troublesome to no one.

And recalling Aelred's style of teaching and preaching, Gilbert explains the reasons for Aelred's wide popularity:

> He abounded in milk-clear teaching for the salvation and consolation of little ones, yet he often slyly mixed with it the wine of a merry and sparkling diction. This is the truth. His milk was as potent as wine. His simple teaching and milk-clear exposition often swept his listener's spirit unaware into the intoxicating transport of a mind beside itself. . . . Indeed he knew how to mix wine deftly in milk and to dispense either one in the other. He chose material easy to work with but you could feel in his words the passion of inebriating grace. He was endowed with a ready understanding but a passionate affection.[52]

Jocelin of Furness's memories of Aelred, written some forty years later, agree:

> He was wholly inspired by a spirit of wisdom and understanding. Moreover, he was a man of the highest integrity, of great practical wisdom, witty and eloquent, a pleasant companion, generous and discreet. And, with all these qualities, he exceeded all his fellow prelates of the Church in his patience and tenderness. He was full of sympathy for the infirmities, both physical and moral, of others.[53]

---

[52]Gilbert, SC 40; PL 184:217–18; CF 26:496–97. Translation by Lawrence C. Braceland sj.

[53]Jocelin, *Acta Sanctorum*, August, i. 257, d, e; quoted from Powicke, p. xxxiii.

Even the *Peterborough Chronicle*, probably written in the fourteenth century, records the passing of Aelred with words of praise for his contributions to the world he had left behind:

> AD 1166. . . . Saint Aelred, abbot of Rievaulx, departed to God. At his death he left behind lands, dwellings, wealth, and church ornaments, all of which had almost doubled in his time, and usages and other spiritual memorials, similarly multiplied.[54]

No evidence exists to suggest that formal steps for the canonization of Aelred were ever planned or taken.[55] The Cistercian Order has, however, long celebrated his feast on the day of his death, 12 January, and in 1476 the General Chapter, in apparent response to the existence in the region of Rievaulx of a local cult of Aelred, authorized a solemn feast of twelve lessons for 'the glorious confessor Aelred'.[56] Most recently, the Episcopal Church in the United States of America in 1991 added his name to the Kalendar as one of those 'whose lives represent heroic commitment to Christ' and 'sanctified in their lives of faith'.[57]

AELRED'S WORKS

In his time Aelred was known in England and beyond as a public figure, the most powerful Cistercian in England, a tireless and affectionate abbot and administrator, an effective mediator, a familiar of hermits, abbots, bishops, and kings. Of that public figure only fragmentary evidence remains: a name in cartularies, an occasional signature on scattered documents, a memory in works of now little-known contemporaries such as Gilbert of Hoyland, Richard of Hexham, Reginald of Durham, and Jocelin of Furness.

---

[54]*Chronicon Angliae Petriburgense*, p. 99: *Item sanctus Alredus abbas Rievallensis migravit ad Dominum, qui terras, et tenementa, opes et ornamenta ecclesiae suae saltem duplicata in tempore suo, mores et alia spiritualia monumenta multiplicata in obitu suo dereliquit.*

[55]See Paul Grosjean, 'La Prétendue Canonisation d'Aelred de Rievaux par Célestin III', *Analecta Bollandiana* 78 (1960) 125–27.

[56]J.-M. Canivez, *Statuta Capitulorum Generalium Ordinis Cisterciensis* (Louvain, 1937) 2.349.

[57]*Lesser Feasts and Fasts* (New York: Church Hymnal Association, 1991) pp. 110–11.

The Aelred known today is primarily the historian, spiritual director, and contemplative theologian who survives in his own writing. For throughout the years of public prominence, as he administered two monasteries, taught and nurtured his monks, and traveled from Dundrennan to Rome and back again, Aelred also wrote prolifically with such simplicity, originality, and power that one would think him to have been always at home. As truly as he was a man of affairs and a man of the Church, he was a man of letters; throughout his monastic life he wrote of events and issues from both worlds.

Aelred's works may be roughly grouped into historical and spiritual subjects, distinct in subject matter and audience. One may sometimes forget Aelred the spiritual director when reading Aelred the historian, while the spiritual treatises, which explore the way to the love of God through love of humankind, seem timeless, ahistorical, as though written by someone without interest in events of the day.

Aelred may have thought of himself as essentially an historian rather than a spiritual writer. His historical works voice none of the resistance to writing of some of the spiritual, and he seems to have been a popular author of saints' lives for ecclesial occasions. Works about and for the secular world contain humor, intellect, and passion for men and women of all sorts and conditions. In them Aelred shows himself as shaped by the world of his ancestors and concerned for the world of twelfth-century England. Watching the strife and bloodshed that tormented the kingdom between 1135 and 1154, as Stephen and Matilda battled for the throne, Aelred, who had grown up on family stories of a similar conflict between the Normans and the heirs of the Anglo-Saxons, began to explore the events and personages of the english past for the benefit of the english present, seeking to guide Henry II both before and during his reign.[58]

[58]For an extended discussion of these works see my introduction to *The Historical Works of Aelred of Rievaulx*, trans. Jane-Patricia Freeland, CF 56 (Kalamazoo: Cistercian—forthcoming); see also Rosalind Ransford, 'A Kind of Noah's Ark: Aelred of Rievaulx and National Identity', ed. Stuart Mews, *Religion and National Identity: Studies in Church History* 18 (1982) 137–46.

Aelred's historical works focus on people rather than the times in which they lived and on the meaning of those people for their twelfth-century descendants. *The Eulogy of King David of Scotland*[59] (1153) mourns the recent death of King David, praises his virtuous reign, and urges that his subjects now give their loyalty, in his memory, to his grandson and heir, Malcolm IV. *The Genealogy of the Kings of England*[60] (1153-54), *The Battle of the Standard*[61] (1155), and *The Life of Saint Edward the Confessor*[62] (1163) all address Henry II either directly or indirectly, praising the virtue of his ancestors and urging him to emulate them. *Genealogy*, written before Henry's reign began, is a mirror for princes, a model for the man who will unite two peoples. *The Battle of the Standard* shows that the best of leaders both cause and endure suffering in war, so urging virtuous rule;[63] the *Life of Saint Edward* declares Henry the cornerstone in which the two walls of the english and norman peoples unite and identifies Edward as his ancestor and patron saint. This last work has had enormous influence on english historical understanding and on the continuing devotion of the english church to the Confessor.[64]

Others of Aelred's works on the history of sanctity in the North of England also concentrate on those who shaped the faith of Scotland and England, again people for whom he had reason to have personal and historical attachment. *The Life of Saint Ninian*[65] (?1154-60), apparently written at the request of a bishop of Whithorn in Galloway, tells of a man whose life in many ways anticipated Aelred's. The most famous of the early saints

[59]PL 195:714–16; Aelred wrote this eulogy at the death of King David in 1153 and then included it in *Genealogy of the Kings of England* as the first chapter.
[60]PL 195:711–38.
[61]PL 195:701–12.
[62]PL 195:737–90.
[63]Antonia Gransden, *Historical Writing in England c. 550 to c. 1307* (Ithaca: Cornell Univ. Press, 1974) pp. 213–16.
[64]Dutton, Portraits, p. 123; Frank Barlow, *Edward the Confessor* (1970; Berkeley: Univ. of California Press, 1984) p. 288; G. E. Moore, *The Middle English Verse Life of Edward the Confessor* (Philadelphia: Univ. of Pennsylvania Press, 1942) pp. xxxiii-lxxi.
[65]W. M. Metcalf, ed., *Pinkerton's Lives of the Scottish Saints* (Paisley, 1889) 1:9–39.

of southern Scotland, this fourth-century Briton was educated at Rome, then returned to Scotland to convert the Picts and to found churches and monasteries. *The Saints of Hexham*, begun apparently for the 1155 translation of the relics of Acca, Alchmund, Frethbert, Tilbert, and Eata in the church at Hexham, records the acts of these great, if now obscure, northern saints as well as some of Wilfrid and Cuthbert, incorporating into them incidents from the history of Aelred's own family. And *The Nun of Watton*[66] (1158-65) records a miraculous incident at a gilbertine house, about which, Aelred says, he was asked to advise.

Although these works concentrate on historical figures and men and women outside the cloister, Aelred's concern to guide Christians to God through the love of humankind appears as well. Repeatedly he directs his readers to imitate their great predecessors—saints and kings and queens—in virtue and faith and to imitate those humble Christians who sought out the saints in trust.

At the same time that Aelred was writing works of history he was also writing popular and widely influential works of spiritual direction, working out a newly incarnational spirituality by means of increasingly sophisticated rhetorical techniques. *The Mirror of Charity*[67] has traditionally been thought, in part because of Walter's comments on it, to have been written in 1142-43, during Aelred's months as novice master at Rievaulx, although Charles Dumont has recently argued persuasively for a date after Aelred became abbot at Revesby, in 1143 or later.[68] This treatise enunciates the relationship between human and divine love, in many ways anticipating the later works of spirituality as well as giving early evidence through its three brief internal dialogues of Aelred's interest in rhetorical innovation, whose technique he was to exploit more fully in *Spiritual Friendship* and *On the Soul*.

Among Aelred's most widely influential works, those in which he began to articulate his incarnational understanding of the route

---

[66]PL 195:789–96.

[67]*De speculo caritatis*, ed. C. H. Talbot, CCCM 1:1–161; CF 17.

[68]Charles Dumont, OCSO, Introduction to *The Mirror of Charity*, CF 17 (Kalamazoo: Cistercian, 1990) pp. 55–59.

to God through human love, are two small treatises of contemplative theology, *On Jesus as a Boy of Twelve*[69] (1153-57) and *On the Institution of Recluses*[70] (1160-62). The first of these explores the gospel narrative of Luke 2:41-52 according to the three traditional levels of medieval allegory. The third portion of the work concerns the contemplative journey to God; there Aelred for the first time teaches meditation on Jesus' life as a way to come to 'the heights of luminous contemplation'.[71]

On the Institution of Recluses, Aelred's single work addressed to a woman, begins as a manual of direction for the anchoritic life, but after the early chapters' rules for the quotidian life of anchoresses, Aelred devotes the larger portion of the work to three meditations intended to stimulate love for Christ. The first of the three, on the sacred humanity of Christ, directs the reader through imaginative intimacy with him in his infancy, childhood, manhood, and Passion to contemplative union with him as Lord. Its influence has been the greatest of all of Aelred's works, having brought about fundamental change in western christian devotion and theology.[72]

The most personal and intimate of Aelred's spiritual works is *Pastoral Prayer*[73] (1163-66), written as illness increasingly restricted the abbot's movement and focused his attention on the community at Rievaulx. Several collections of sermons also survive; one group of these, *On the Burdens of Isaiah*[74] (1158-63), is dedicated to Gilbert Foliot, bishop of London.

---

[69]*De Iesu puero duodenni*, ed. Anselm Hoste, CCCM 1:245–78; 'Jesus at the Age of Twelve', trans. Theodore Berkeley, OCSO, *Treatises; The Pastoral Prayer,* CF 2 (Kalamazoo: Cistercian Publications, 1971) pp. 3–39.

[70]*De institutione inclusarum*, ed. C. H. Talbot, CCCM 1:635–82; 'A Rule of Life for a Recluse', trans. Mary Paul Macpherson, OCSO, *Treatises; The Pastoral Prayer,* CF 2 (Kalamazoo: Cistercian, 1971) pp. 41–102.

[71]Jesu 3.19; CCCM 1:266; CF 2:26.

[72]I have discussed the wide influence of Aelred's meditative approach in 'The Cistercian Source: Aelred, Bonaventure, and Ignatius', *Goad and Nail: Studies in Medieval Cistercian History, X,* ed. E. Rozanne Elder, CS 84 (Kalamazoo: Cistercian, 1984) pp. 151–78. See also J. Maréchal, 'Application des Sens', *Dictionnaire de Spiritualité,* 1 (1937) 823–24.

[73]CCCM 1:755–63; ET CF 2:103–18.

[74]PL 195:361–500. Gaetano Raciti is editing all redactions of Aelred's surviving sermons for CCCM; the first volume appeared in 1989 as *Aelredi Rievallen-*

Aelred's last works of spirituality move in a new direction, away from pastoral guidance to topics more abstract and speculative, more concerned with moral and theological inquiry than with spiritual direction, though still exploring the soul's movement toward God in this life and the next. Aelred composed both *On the Soul*[75] (1163-66) and *Spiritual Friendship*[76] (1164-67) as ciceronian dialogues, constructing a dramatic explication that divides the argument of the works into discrete blocks of thought and leads the reader through each step in its logic with the help of the participants in the dialogue, always an abbot-teacher and one or several monk-learners. *On the Soul*, an exploration of the implications of augustinian psychology, seeks to explain the nature of God through greater understanding of the nature of the human soul, suggesting: 'Perhaps, when you have found the image, you will more easily find him of whom it is the image'.[77] Although Walter Daniel reports that this work remained unfinished at Aelred's death (42), it seems complete in both argument and form.

Finally, *Spiritual Friendship* powerfully brings together Aelred's historical and spiritual concerns, his desire to write for and about those both inside and outside the monastery. Its two primary sources are Cicero's *On Friendship* and Augustine's *Confessions*, and its examples of spiritual friendships are drawn from both history and literature; it thus ties together themes and texts from Aelred's secular and theological education. A contemporary example of false friendship involving Octavian of Monticello, antipope Victor IV from 1159 until his death in 1164,[78] provides the *terminus a quo* of the work. This rare revelation in a spiritual treatise of Aelred's concern with events outside the monastery not only assists in dating the work but shows the final literary integration of the

sis Sermones I-XLVI: Collectio Claraevallensis Prima et Secunda, CCCM 2A (Turnholt: Brepols, 1989).

[75]*Dialogus de anima*, ed. C. H. Talbot, CCCM 1:683–754; *Dialogue on the Soul*, trans. C. H. Talbot, CF 22 (Kalamazoo: Cistercian, 1981).

[76]*De spiritali amicitia*, ed. Anselm Hoste and C. H. Talbot, CCCM 1:279–350. *Spiritual Friendship*, trans. M. Eugenia Laker SSND, CF 5 (Kalamazoo: Cistercian, 1974).

[77]Anima 5; CCCM 1:686; CF 22:37.

[78]Spir amic 2.41; CCCM 1:310; CF 5:79–80.

historical and spiritual, worldly and cenobitic concerns of his life and work.

The desire to identify the sources used by Walter Daniel in compiling his Life of Aelred has apparently plagued readers since the work appeared, according to the Letter to Maurice, where Walter both objects to the question of his sources and identifies witnesses to Aelred's miracles. Although Walter has little to say on the topic in the *Vita,* its concentration on the final years of Aelred's life and Walter's ubiquity in the story of those years suggest that he is his own primary source. Yet Walter insists that his witness is supported by the report of others. In the *Vita* he writes:

> I set limits to my grasp of the miracles and works of the father, I bow to their infinity, and tell only those which are common knowledge, whose truth is well established and proved by the long experience of those whose praiseworthy life testifies to the truth of their evidence. If this were not so I should prefer complete silence to doubtful truth. Everything I say I saw myself or give from the account of eye-witnesses. Wherefore, since our story is confirmed by the testimony not of two or three but of many religious, pious readers should hold it so much the more dear, as no vestige of error will mar their apprehension of it. (48-9)

And in the Letter he writes: 'The powers of belief in the hearts of the faithful might have been satisfied by my assertion that I have written only the things which I had seen or what others had seen and told me, but those two prelates accept nothing that is not attested by formal and public proof' (69).

Walter's primary source, however, is surely Aelred himself, at the time of the *Vita*'s publication no longer available to vouch for its accuracy. Walter seems to have first heard many of the early stories from Aelred, as he explicitly states regarding Aelred's first miracle of prayer, the case of the novice ('with no mental stability') who left Rievaulx but found himself brought home again by nightfall by Aelred's prayer (24):

Moreover, the venerable father Aelred told me about this miracle, not as a miracle, because of his humility, but, because of
my own deficiency, as a remarkable happening (67).

Aelred may also have been the source for the narrative of his
conversion, although its curious and significant gaps in Walter's
telling—the nature of Aelred's business with Archbishop Thurstan
of York, the name of the friend who mentioned the new house of
white monks—suggests that Walter reconstructed its broad outlines
from memory.

Other stories from Aelred's early years, especially those of his
years at David's court, seem equally likely to have come to Walter
from Aelred. The story of Aelred's averting a jealous knight's anger
by his humble response and his consequent winning of the angry
man to friendship (5-7) sounds so much like a personal homiletic
instance of the power of peace against wrath—one with particular
relevance to the irascible Walter—that Aelred may have told it to
Walter also 'because of [his] own deficiency' (67).

Some of these chapters also point to Walter's efforts to reconstruct the growth of Aelred's mind and spirit in those early years
from the evidence of his works. Chapter 10, on Aelred's life of
meditation, for example, tells of his pouring out his mind 'like a
flood upon God and his Son', reflecting on the Passion, Creation,
Fall, Redemption, Hell, and Heaven (19). As it was the great
cistercian writers, including Aelred himself, who so powerfully
turned the attention of the christian West to the sacred humanity
of Christ and specifically to the Passion, and as these are the
subjects of Aelred's meditations in *On the Institution of Recluses,* it
seems less likely that Aelred in the 1130s was already exploring the
topics that would come to flower in his works of thirty years later
than that in the 1160s Walter Daniel attempted to reconstruct the
spiritual history of the novice of three decades earlier by examining
his later works.

The chapters on Aelred as novice master must also reflect
Walter's later knowledge of Aelred and familiarity with his work,
especially as it is in these pages that Walter identifies himself
as having served as Aelred's scribe. As it is in this section that
Walter writes of Aelred's authorship of *The Mirror of Charity,* it

is natural for him at this point to praise Aelred's fine mind and his simple, unlearned rhetoric. But his treatment of Aelred's spirit and mind, though arranged according to the stages in Aelred's life, consistently represents Walter's seventeen years of acquaintance with the abbot of Rievaulx and his works and primarily the last four of those years.

Walter occasionally mentions outside sources in the *Vita*, though rarely by name. He cites the testimony of the aged Simon, abbot of Sartis, who had been Aelred's novice master, about the young monk's life of contemplation, prayer, and labor (16-18), appeals to those who were novices under Aelred as bearing witness 'as much by the sweetness of their character as by the living voice to his praiseworthy industry' (23), and tells of 'a certain religious brother' who received a vision conveying the truth that Aelred would not die until cleansed for immediate admission to beatitude (52-54). Naming Richard, abbot of Fountains, and Roger, abbot of Byland, as present at Aelred's death, he implicitly appeals to their verification of his account.

In the Letter to Maurice Walter finally indignantly names witnesses to all the miracles of the *Vita,* citing a variety of figures from Rievaulx and elsewhere:

> Henry and Robert, both of Beverley, monks and priests; Ralph the deacon, called the Short, himself a well-proved monk . . . the lord Gospatric, our monk and priest . . . the lord Daniel my father, Geoffrey the sacristan . . . William Ruffus, monk and priest, and Martin the deacon . . . Ralph of Rothwell, priest and monk . . . Arnold, at one time our cellarer, . . . Thomas of York, a young deacon of good life and a son of holy conversation. . . . Robert our under-porter, a good and excellent man. (67-69)

In this list he also names those who benefited from Aelred's miracles and finally, with regard to the healing of the man who had swallowed a frog, concludes extravagantly 'and almost more persons in Galloway than can be numbered' (69).

In defending the *Vita's* description of Aelred's death and the beauty of his body in death, Walter in the letter also cites earlier authors, mentioning specifically Sulpicius Severus's *Life of Saint*

Martin (77). He thus reveals not only his own almost instinctive use of standard rhetorical and hagiographical works but his expectation that his readers will recognize such use. He provides his citations, like the names of witnesses whose testimony will substantiate his miraculous stories, as evidence of having followed the conventions of hagiography: far from responding with embarrassment at having described Aelred's body in language taken from that previously used of Saint Martin's, with the possible implication that perhaps Aelred's body was not 'clearer than glass, whiter than snow' (62), he confidently cites his authority as proof that hyperbole in such an instance is not only recommended by rhetoricians but validated by previous use.[79]

THE *VITA AELREDI*

Although Walter develops the *Vita Aelredi* in a roughly chronological order, his literary model, as he acknowledges in the Letter to Maurice, is the saint's life. He shows little interest in the exterior events of Aelred's life; his explicit purpose is to celebrate and commemorate the humility and charity of his abbot and so to present him as a moral exemplar. Repeatedly he returns to this point, explaining in the prefatory letter his desire to show Aelred's sanctity to 'those who, thirsting in spirit, are wont to embrace examples of the good' (2) and referring to Aelred as a youth at David's court as 'this pattern among men' (7).

At the same time the work seems more a eulogy, a commemoration of the recently departed abbot of Rievaulx, than a work intended to establish him as a saint. It focuses on his monastic life, his virtues, and his love for his monks and for God, and while Walter records a number of miracles from Aelred's monastic life, these reveal more his love and prayer for his spiritual sons and their reliance upon him than they do supernatural powers. While Walter insists on Aelred's 'outshining sanctity' (2), he does not suggest continuing power from beyond the grave. The work

[79]See Heffernan, pp. 111–16.

resembles Aelred's eulogy for King David of Scotland more than his lives of Saints Ninian and Edward.

The *Vita* is primarily a commemorative portrait of Aelred the monk and abbot, emphasizing his remarkable humility, patience, charity, wisdom, and spiritual strength. Although Walter claims that these virtues characterized Aelred long before he entered monastic life, the work offers little information about his early life, and the public signs and fruits of his combined virtue and piety appear, by degrees, only after he becomes abbot of Revesby. The *Vita* provides no information about Aelred's childhood, and only twice does Walter mention his family, referring to the Rievaulx sub-cellarer as 'his nearest kinsman' (31) and identifying the audience of *On the Institution of Recluses* as his sister (41). He gives no explanation for the anomaly of a northumbrian priest's son's spending his adolescent years at the scottish court and shows little interest in Aelred's secular education.

Further, despite Walter's particular interest in Aelred's *Spiritual Friendship,* the *Vita* has nothing to say about friendships Aelred may have had before or after entering Rievaulx except to tell of a jealous knight at David's court, who was so transformed by Aelred's example that 'he promised to be Aelred's firm friend in the future' (8). The other young people at court remain at best shadowy figures, in Walter's eyes irrelevant to Aelred's life during those years and afterward. Unlike Aelred's own works, whose references to friends and events at court have prompted countless biographical forays, the *Vita* offers almost no material about Aelred's ten years with David except the nature and value of his service to David and its moral and spiritual benefits.

While Walter provides some information about Aelred's office at David's court, he says next to nothing about his public life after becoming a monk. Aelred barely exists for Walter outside the monastery; references to his visits elsewhere are brief and tied to monastic business or, vaguely, preaching 'in our chapters, in synods and to the people'. (42)

The structure of the *Vita* calls particular attention to Walter's concern with Aelred's humility, charity, and piety—his sanctity—within monastic life. The work is throughout shaped to reflect

Walter's purposes, with the great themes accented and aspects of Aelred's life that are either irrelevant or contradictory to those purposes ignored. Of the work's fifty-nine chapters, only three tell of Aelred's life before conversion, and one of those focuses on his growing desire while at court to enter monastic life. Another three chapters narrate his conversion. Twenty-three chapters tell of his life from 1134 through 1157, during which he entered Rievaulx, served as novice master, became abbot at Revesby, returned to Rievaulx as abbot, and served the first half of his abbacy. The final half of the work presents, in thirty chapters, the last ten years of his life, during which, according to Walter, the General Chapter relieved him of many of his abbatial responsibilities. Of those thirty chapters, twenty are devoted to his last four years, thirteen to his last year and death.

Within this chronological structure Walter develops the principal theme of his work: Aelred's sanctity, the way in which Aelred integrated piety, virtue (epitomized by his patience and charity), and wisdom and manifested those gifts of grace in building up monastic communities, writing letters, treatises, and sermons, doing miracles, and dying in *imitatio Christi*. Walter integrates the various aspects of Aelred's sanctity into the work, but his placement argues for Aelred's growth in spiritual power over his lifetime and especially during his monastic career. And although in the course of the work Walter writes of the many faces of virtue in Aelred—his prudence, his mildness, his purity—he returns always to those two that defined the abbot's life from its earliest days: humility and charity. He cites Aelred's novice master's memory that in Aelred's earliest days in monastic life, while still a novice, 'he excelled all his comrades and fellow-soldiers in humility and glowed in piety. . . . The most remarkable thing in one who exceeded all in the other virtues was a charity, which won the victory over himself' (17).

From its beginning the *Vita* insists on Aelred's piety and virtue as combining in sanctity. The prefatory letter insists on his 'life and character', 'the charity and astonishing sanctity of so great a father', and 'the outshining sanctity of him who . . . showed himself a father to the brethren' (1-2). The Life proper begins with sentences declaring Aelred to have been marked by both virtue and devotion to God in the first stages of his life, his boyhood (*puericia*) and youth (*adolescencia*). Throughout these early years, Walter says, Aelred was already set apart by extraordinary virtue, 'and the vices of manhood were not possible in him' (2). Furthermore, unlike most young men, he had already in his youth begun 'to meditate on God and to perfect his holy meditations with works' (2). The relationship between Aelred's meditation and his life of virtue is thus established in the second sentence of the Life.

The virtue and piety Aelred showed in childhood also characterized his life at court. Walter quickly moves from the power Aelred exercised there 'as a second lord and prince over a host of officials and all the men of the court' (3) to an encomium of David as an exemplar of piety and virtue for the young Aelred. He emphasizes Aelred's prudence and justice and draws attention to the parallel between Aelred's early service to his secular king and his life-long service to the king of heaven. Despite being already set apart from the world, Walter says, Aelred was willing temporarily to serve at court because David was 'a lord so pure and holy, a man whose life inspired a veneration due to it, a king whose authority gave strength to it' (2).

But while David served as an example of virtuous life in the world, Walter insists that the young Aelred's true teacher and source of virtue even at court was God: 'God had taught him patience and had enriched his active spirit with no little prudence' (4). Even as Aelred served at the royal table, 'his thoughts would be in the other world, and oblivious to outward things, as one caught up in an ecstasy to the heavenly heights, he would forget the affairs of the belly in a pleasant excess of contemplation of the apostolic words' (4).

During those years at court, then, Aelred was already marked by the traits that would characterize the rest of his life. All that he did was marked with mildness; he was just and peaceful, patient and prudent: 'Throughout his life he took pains to return love for hate, good for evil, kindness for envy, the gracious word and the friendly deed for ill-speaking' (5). Even at court he lived ascetically, making 'his vesture into a symbol and forecast of the admirable poverty of his later life' (5).

As Aelred in young adulthood exercised responsibility over David's court, so at Rievaulx and briefly at Revesby he was to combine personal humility, patience, and charity with the exercise of authority and justice. In drawing the parallel, Walter suggests that Aelred's very name fitted him for such office:

> The great counsellor had a fitting name, for the English *Alred* is in Latin *totum consilium* or *omne consilium*. Well is he placed in the counsels of an earthly king, whose very name gives forth the sound, 'all counsel', he who was afterwards to be father, counsellor, judge and protector of many servants of God, first showing an example of justice to his companions in the world, then in loftier regions of a more exacting life the pattern even to spiritual men of perfection and inward humility. (8)[80]

Aelred's first twenty-four years serve in Walter's narrative to establish the pattern of his adult life.

As the early chapters of the *Vita* set forth Aelred in his service to David and his conversion from the secular world to the monastic, where he will for thirty-three years live and where he will die, they also begin to establish a tension and balance between the two worlds in which Aelred spent his life: 'the religious life of an accepted kind' (*cuiuslibet probate professionis*) and 'the vainglory of this wicked life' (9-10). As Walter tells the story, Aelred began to yearn for monastic life while still in David's service, but hesitated to tell him 'lest he should be disturbed by his fear for his lord and suffer delays' (10). But God was calling Aelred from the court to monastic life, Walter insists, not for his own well-being but for that of others:

> God willed that for the welfare and comfort of many he should give himself more strictly to the way of quiet and holiness and, so to speak, enter into his chamber where the floods of the evil world do not flow . . . where a new song is sung, the song of Sion, and a continual Alleluia . . . ; God willing, I say, by his

---

[80]The anglo-saxon form of Aelred's name, *Aethelred* 'noble counsel' would have been equally appropriate for Walter's purposes.

grace to call his servant to this laudable and happy state, inspired him. . . . (9)

Thus despite failing to tell David of his desire, Aelred found himself, while on a royal mission to York, at Rievaulx.

In Walter's report Aelred's response to God's call is not merely one of obedience, but of a readiness for heavenly things that shaped his youthful experience. Hearing of the new settlement of white monks, Walter recounts, 'he exclaimed, "And where, o where, is the way to those angelic men, to these heavenly places?" (13). After a night's visit with Walter Espec, who told him 'still more about the life of the monks', he spent the next day at Rievaulx 'listening to the monks talk of spiritual things' (14).

Having shown Aelred's readiness to answer God's call, Walter complements it with his humility, seen in an unwillingness to put his will before that of others. After another night's conversation and sleep at the castle of Walter Espec, on the next morning Aelred, 'still aflame with the Holy Spirit, that is to say, with the love of the Lord Jesus', set out for Scotland. But as he rode on the flat way above the steep passage leading down to the monastery, he was seized with the desire to return and asked one of his servants, 'whom he called his friend', says Walter, 'if he would like to go down to the abbey.' This final step in Aelred's turning toward monastic life reveals the whole. For Walter, God's mercy and Aelred's humility work together for good:

> Oh, the mercy of our God, ever to be proclaimed by those who wish to make their home in Christ! Oh, how faithful is our God in clemency and kindness! . . . Take note here of the outshining humility of this gentlest of men, whose own will depended on the will of his servant. God indeed opened the mouth of that servant. He said, 'I am for going down,' and what the servant preferred to do the lord decided should be done. So they went down to the monastery of Rievaulx. (15)

Walter not only presents Aelred's conversion as the symbolic center, the turning point, of his life, but shows this critical moment as shaped by the features that are part of his whole life of sanctity, in childhood, youth, maturity, and age. But while the conversion is a turning from one world, one kind of service, to another,

Aelred himself changes not at all in the process. He merely comes home to the place where he can direct his service at last to his heavenly king.

In the six chapters on Aelred's years as a novice, Walter shows him as characterized by the same piety and virtues as those that had served him so well at court, but now as well by 'the three marks of monastic life, holy contemplation, prayer, and honest toil' (18). Three chapters examine each of these three aspects of his life, while a fourth notes his ability to combine the 'honey of the contemplation by which he drank in the pleasures of heaven, the oil of piety which made him shine, the butter of compassion for his neighbor, for whose sins he poured out his prayers to God' (22). Walter also shows Aelred's purity through his renewed asceticism as he builds a cold-water bath beneath the novice-house in order to 'quench the heat in himself of every vice' (25). Walter first here praises his intelligence, not yet matured into wisdom, but inherent in 'his fine and acute mind' and 'natural capacity to a high degree' (26), his knowledge of the liberal arts, his rhetorical style of purity and simplicity, and his first work of spiritual guidance, *The Mirror of Charity*.

While Walter points to the virtuous aspects of Aelred's character throughout the work and returns to them especially in the portions devoted to his abbacy, in these early chapters he is intent to show the benefits they brought to the monasteries rather than their role in Aelred's own life or even in his ability to counsel or teach others. As at court Aelred's virtue and attention to the things of God had brought him the confidence of David and, at length, the respect and affection of all, so his many years of monastic governance brought about even more evident fruits, made visible in the growth and well-being of his communities.

To Revesby and Rievaulx, Walter says, Aelred brought both economic prosperity and 'intensity of the monastic life and its charity'. He attracted new members to the community at Revesby, developed its religious life, and at the same time enthusiastically acquired property, money, and equipment. At Rievaulx he not only insisted that 'it is the singular and supreme glory of the house of Rievaulx that above all else it teaches tolerance of the infirm and compassion with others in their necessities', but 'his material legacy was great enough, under prudent management, to feed and clothe a still greater number [than the 640 who Walter says were there], and to leave something over for their successors' (37–38). The prosperity of both monasteries, Walter implies, came first of all because of Aelred's charity; material success was a proof of Aelred's sanctity.

Walter also insists on Aelred's wisdom as teacher, preacher, and writer. He reports that while master of novices, Aelred 'began to write to various personages letters most lucid in sense and distinguished in style' and wrote *The Mirror of charity*, which Walter praises as 'what in my judgement is the best of all his works . . . , which contains as good a picture of the love of God and one's neighbor as a man can see of himself in a mirror' (25–6).

This passage, coming within a lengthy discussion of Aelred as a teacher and writer, indicates that Aelred while still a young monk was involving himself in affairs of the world beyond the cloister. It also suggests that Aelred wrote both the letters and the treatise at his own initiative. The tradition that Bernard directed the unwilling Aelred to write *The Mirror of Charity*, borne out by Bernard's letter overruling his hesitance, was apparently, in light of this passage, unknown to Walter.[81] At the time that Aelred wrote this first work, Walter was not yet at Rievaulx, not yet Aelred's scribe, so he could not know from his own experience of Bernard's role. Aelred must never have mentioned to Walter either his initial resistance to the task or Bernard's instruction.

[81]The thirteenth-century Anchin manuscript of *Speculum caritatis* (Douai Bib. Mun. MS 392) contains Bernard's letter on f. 2ᵛ, facing the beginning of Aelred's treatise. In the upper left corner of Bernard's letter an initial E pictures Bernard himself sitting in the heavens, his hair and beard of blue matching the sky against which he is pictured. He leans forward down and across the page, holding a scroll toward the initial at the bottom right of f. 3ʳ, in which Aelred (identified as 'Ailred *monacho*') sits, apparently on the ground, holding a scroll and looking up toward Bernard. Although the initial showing Aelred has been often reproduced in isolation, it is only one half of a tableau portraying the two as though in dialogue; the scene visually preserves the tradition of a humble Aelred's writing in obedience to the command of his exalted spiritual father.

In introducing Aelred as a writer of letters and treatises at this early point in the narrative of his life, however, Walter is more concerned with their bearing on Aelred's mind, education, and rhetorical approach than with the works themselves, apparently because of his own energetic rhetorical opinions. As an educated man and himself a writer it is not surprising that Walter should have had opinions on the subject; he expresses especially enthusiastic praise for Aelred's use of a simple written style to convey the truth: 'He despised the vain pursuit of eloquence and preferred the pure, undiluted truth of the matter about which he might be speaking' (27). So he insists that Aelred's life of simplicity, truth, and virtue was manifest in all he wrote and that his works were themselves the fruits of his virtue and piety.

Walter again discusses Aelred as writer within the narrative of the last ten years of his life, as he lived in his cottage (*tugurium*), talking with 'the brethren [who] . . . every day came to it and sat in it, twenty or thirty at a time, to talk together of the spiritual delights of the Scripture and of the observance of the Order' (40). It was during this time and in this place, Walter says, that Aelred became a writer of works for spiritual guidance. He identifies Aelred at this point in his life as not merely a writer of rhetorical excellence and simplicity of life, but as a man of wisdom fit for teaching by speech and written word: 'it was in that private closet [*secretario*] that he wrote and finished with his own hand the thirty-three homilies on the burden of Babylon, in Isaiah, and after these, other fine and profitable works' (41).

Walter names and summarizes these other works—*Spiritual Friendship, On the Institution of Recluses, The Life of Saint Edward, King and Confessor,* a homily on Luke 11:33 for the Confessor's translation, and *On the Soul*—then adds that Aelred wrote as well 'about two hundred most eloquent sermons' and letters, 'in which he left a living image of himself, for what he there commended in writing he himself practised in life, and lived much better than he could say' (42). Thus he shows that while Aelred taught members of the community at Rievaulx during these last years, he wrote as well for the instruction of those outside the community, offering to all insight that emerged from and was shaped by his life of prayer and contemplation, of patience and humility, of love for God and neighbor.

Finally for Walter it is the miracles that Aelred accomplished in the course of his monastic life that best reveal the spiritual reality within his deeds and words. After telling of his many letters and sermons, Walter endeavors to place in proper order the signs and benefits of his sanctity:

> Such, then, were the fruits put forth by the venerable father, and just as many miracles, of which I now proceed to give a faithful account, are associated with him. For I deem it unjust to show to the readers of this work the brick, wood, brass and iron in which the father abounded in external things, and to be silent about the silver, gold and precious stones in which his spirit exceeded. (42)

Although virtue and piety were prominent at each stage of Aelred's life, their miraculous effects began only after he became novice master at Rievaulx, and only toward the end of his life did the power given him to heal and see into the future become fully developed.

Walter presents the growth of Aelred's wonder-working abilities systematically and economically. While his loving prayer is at all stages equally efficacious, its power over nature and the human spirit becomes stronger in each stage of his life and truly miraculous only after he becomes an abbot. Similarly his power to heal, which apparently develops during his first abbacy, increases geometrically during his second: two healings occur at Revesby, four at Rievaulx. The difference has nothing to do with the fact that Aelred spent twenty years at Rievaulx and only four at Revesby; Walter is interested not in the miracles or their numbers but in what they reveal about the life and growing spiritual power of this man through whom God acts. Finally, only toward the end of his life does Aelred become able to exercise prophetic vision for the benefit of his spiritual sons and, perhaps, to curse.

By the experience of one man, a secular clerk who enters Rievaulx while Aelred is novice master, Walter exemplifies the increasing power of Aelred's prayer and Aelred's first experience of prophetic vision. The simplicity of this arrangement enables

Walter to concentrate on the change taking place in Aelred rather than being distracted by accidental differences among those for whom he prays. The clerk who three times benefits from Aelred's prayer thereby becomes a familiar figure, with a personal history by which Walter can each time reintroduce him. He represents all the individual monks, all Aelred's spiritual sons who do not become individually known to the reader.

The repeated appearance of this man, always with the same purpose and essentially the same effect, makes manifest the development of Aelred's spiritual power. Aelred prays for him once while novice master at Rievaulx, once while abbot at Revesby, and a third time while abbot at Rievaulx. In each case the monk, 'a man with no mental stability' (24), wishes to leave the monastery, and in each case Aelred's prayer prevents him. The first time he leaves the grounds but comes back at nightfall; the second time Aelred's prayer raises a wall of air against his departure; and the third time, although he is outside the monastery and seeking to visit his family before returning, Aelred is able to bring him back inside.

The first of these events is presented not really as a miracle by Walter, but as evidence of 'the compassion in his heart and his perfection in religious life'; the story continues, however, with the admonition 'let those hear who wish to hear what he did, or rather what God, working through him, did, for a certain brother' (24). And Walter concludes the story with the words: 'through Aelred's sincerity in prayer, that brother ended his life clothed in his sacred habit, in Aelred's hands' (25).[82] As Walter has shown Aelred the novice master as already a writer marked by a fine mind but not yet characterized by wisdom and the power of spiritual counsel, his prayers too are not yet able to work miracles: as yet Aelred merely prays sincerely, as any novice master, any monk, any lover of God might do. But as Aelred progresses in monastic life, his spiritual

---

[82]Walter apparently considers it a miraculous event at the time he writes, however, as in the Letter he refers to it as such before explaining that Aelred 'because of his humility' told it to him 'not as a miracle . . . but . . . as a remarkable happening' (67).

powers increase accordingly. When the unstable monk seeks to leave Revesby, Abbot Aelred's prayer, by raising 'the empty air as though it were a wall of iron', prevents his departure. Walter explicitly calls this incident miraculous (32).

The third intervention on behalf of this man, and the first of Aelred's prophetic visions, seems to have taken place soon after Aelred became abbot of Rievaulx. Warned in a dream of the imminent death of this monk, he goes to meet him on his return from a mission outside the monastery and resists his plea to delay his entry into the monastery; then 'with fair words he enticed the monk to come into the monastery with him'. When after a few days the monk fell ill, Aelred, in fulfillment of his dream, 'taking the head in his hands, exclaimed "Saint Benedict, pray for him"' (35-6). So this monk who had throughout his monastic life sought release found it at last, in the hands of him who had from the beginning of that life loved him and cared for his soul.

Aelred's ability to heal comes about only after he has become an abbot, and Walter is careful to note that the basis of that ability is his holiness and his merits. At Revesby Aelred heals his wasted sub-prior with a word, commanding: 'in the name of the Lord, make your way to the church, take your place in the choir of the psalmodists, sing with them and pray to God, and through Him, I believe, you will be well' (30). Afterward, Walter says, the cured sub-prior clings 'in ever-growing affection to the holiness, proved for his sake, of the father' (30). Aelred's second miracle at Revesby is accomplished not by word or act, but by the power resident in his crozier. A monk who is a craftsman is healed of a crippling injury 'by the merits of the blessed man' when he passes Aelred's abbatial staff three times about his arm (32). After Aelred becomes abbot at Rievaulx, however, he becomes truly a worker of miracles. He heals one monk and one shepherd— probably a lay-brother—of muteness, restores a monk about to die of heart failure, and brings forth a frog from a young man who had swallowed it as a tadpole in a cup of water.

While Aelred is developing new power for the benefit of his monks, they are growing in devotion and obedience to him; it is largely through their mutual love and respect that the miraculous takes place. Aelred's intercession for the unstable monk is effective as a direct result of his character and his love for the son for whose soul and salvation he is responsible, an outcome of the charity through which he leads and shapes the monastic community. Walter thus shows that the true power of God is to be seen in the love of human beings for one another, the friend for the friend, the abbot for his monk. The miracle is in the eye of faith.

The miracles of healing similarly arise from the mutual love and respect between Aelred and his monks and from Aelred's charity and compassion for both members and non-members of his community. Aelred cures the wasted sub-prior while on a routine visit to the infirmary; he heals him, Walter says, because he 'utterly refuses to allow such a loss to the house, and such a distressing state of body' (30). Aelred is unmistakably here the compassionate but firm superior of the community who refuses to accede to passivity unto death, understanding that one who has given up on life can best regain health of body and spirit by returning to work. Similarly the most powerful and moving image in the case of a young man dying of a heart ailment is not the misery of the youth or the miraculous healing, but Walter's memory of the aged abbot, hastening from the darkened orchard to save the life of his son: 'Night had set in, and you could discern the old man stumbling along, seeking no aid of the staff which he always used' (43). Aelred becomes real here rather than an abstract and holy figure. Walter shows him as most miraculous, most spiritually graced, in his concern and love for his sons, in the charity that neglects his own needs because of those of others.

The healing of a young man grossly distended from swallowing a frog makes the same point, emphasizing not Aelred's miraculous powers but his remarkable charity (and in the Letter Walter refers to it as 'this miracle, or, if you prefer, likeness of a miracle' [68]). Aelred's ability to cure in this instance comes precisely because of his compassion, which Walter sharply though tacitly contrasts with his own horror at the sight: 'his head itself was sunk into his monstrous body without any sign of a neck. In his swollen condition the man appeared like a very fat ox or sheep . . . he was a terrifying object to everybody' (46-47).[83] Aelred, however, not only speaks gently to the young man, asking the cause of his malady, but puts his fingers into his mouth and extracts the frog.

The prophetic insight that characterizes Aelred's last years reveals another kind of miraculous power, resulting from his experience of celestial visitation. Become 'worthy of the spirit of prophecy' (51), Aelred sees the return and forthcoming death of the unstable monk, tells the brothers of sins they have done in secret and orders them to confess, and recognizes the presence of the devil in the dormitory from a report of two monks' shouting during the night. Walter thus insists that Aelred's spiritual power is seen not only in his ability to heal but in his knowledge and understanding. Even while bedridden he remains knowledgeable about and concerned for the spiritual health of the community; his physical isolation from the activity of the monastery does not isolate him emotionally, intellectually, or spiritually. He remains until his death the father and abbot of his monks.

Although Walter presents Aelred's prophetic visions and miracles as 'the silver, gold and precious stones in which his spirit exceeded' (42), they are not themselves the riches, but the outward illumination of the riches that are Aelred's charity. In the Letter to Maurice Walter explains:

> Our father's are great miracles. But bad men can work miracles, even great miracles. True, but only good men have the perfect charity of Aelred. . . . without charity whatever a man may do goes for nothing, even though he can can hang the mass of the terrestrial universe upon one finger. Charity is a fine thing, a sweet thing, a lovable thing, a thing which never lacks the rewarding fruit of eternal graciousness. . . . I marvel at the charity of Aelred more than I should marvel if he had raised four men from the dead. . . . Aelred's charity . . . exceeded every novelty of miracle. (78)

In this portrait, then, as Aelred's 'charity and astonishing sanctity' are identical, his miracles are merely the sign of his charity, his love for all in need made manifest.

---

[83]Powicke finds Walter's 'pathological extravaganza' so excessive that he abbreviates it in his translation (p. 47n).

Aelred's power is not altogether beneficent, however. As Walter claims for his abbot the power to heal bodies and to save from death, he also once attributes to him the power to curse and to consign to death. When insulted by the abbot of a daughter house, whom Maurice Powicke identifies as probably Hugh of Revesby,[84] Aelred in anger cries out to God, asking that 'this man . . . speedily suffer an end to his malice' (44). Almost as soon as the visiting abbot returns home, 'without the blessing of the venerable father Aelred', he becomes ill, dying in seven days (44-45).

While power to curse is familiar in saints' lives from the twelfth century,[85] Walter was reasonably enough uneasy with this aspect of his portrait of Aelred. In the Letter to Maurice he reconsiders the incident, although his critics seem not to have objected to it, and he refuses to name any witnesses, saying that while all that he said was true, 'it is possible that the abbot . . . did not die for the reason for which it seems he died' (68). The interest of this passage is not so much whether the angry abbot died because of the curse, but whether the Aelred whose Life Walter is writing would ever have reacted so harshly to insult, whether the reaction is true to Aelred and to Walter's understanding of him. Gilbert of Hoyland described Aelred after his death as: 'Quick to listen, slow to speak, but not slow to anger. How is he to be described as slow to anger? I would rather say he was not in the race!'[86] Certainly the incident is inconsistent with everything else known about Aelred. It contradicts Walter's insistence on his humility and patience and suggests that whereas as the young Aelred had been not only patient but wise enough to dispel the anger of a jealous knight, in age he became irritable and impetuous, easily provoked to answer anger with anger. Walter's tardy second thoughts suggest that the version in the *Vita* may have emerged more from his own anger at the discourtesy of the visiting abbot and his own satisfied judgment of the appropriateness of his subsequent death than from any words of Aelred.

[84]Powicke, p. lxx.
[85]E.g., *Wulfric of Haselbury, by John, Abbot of Ford*, ed. Maurice Bell, Somerset Record Society 47 (London: SRS, 1933) pp. 61–63. Translation by +Eugene Green and Beverly Mayne Kienzle, forthcoming from Cistercian Publications.
[86]SC 40 [PL 41:4]; PL 184:217; CF 26:496.

Aelred's sanctity in Walter's portrait consists in his asceticism, his patience, humility, and charity, his accomplishment of economic and spiritual prosperity at two monasteries, his gift of spiritual guidance through personal example, preaching, conversation, letters, treatises, and miracles. But the dying abbot's immersion in spiritual reading and his contemplative experience finally prove that sanctity. During his final years, while he endures great suffering, counsels the monks of Rievaulx, and writes treatises of spiritual guidance, Aelred receives the spiritual rewards his love has sought. Although he has shown virtue and piety in childhood, youth, and adulthood and has done miracles throughout his years as abbot, only in age and great illness—in the last four years of his life—does he receive heavenly confirmation of the divine love that holds him and the certainty of beatitude that he awaits.

In his last four years, Walter says, Aelred, 'taking his soul in his hands, gave greater weight to his own counsels than to those of the physicians, and for God's sake despised the cure of the body and considered in all ways the health of the soul' (50). He spent his time in reading, prayer, and contemplation, no longer resisting temptation in a cold-water bath in his cell but sitting 'in a kind of grave in the floor of the little oratory' and calling out for the end of his darkness. And in response, Walter says, 'often, throughout those four years, so some declare for a fact', God sent him light and company:

> the light of angelic visitation shone there upon his head and he talked with heavenly spirits just as he was wont to speak with men; and when he was alone there, many voices used to be heard there, and that place became very dreadful. These visitations of divine grace and angelic conversations made a new man of him, and . . . he revealed by the colour of his countenance and a change in his face that he had been in the presence of spiritual agencies of the divine light and had contemplated heavenly visions. (50-51)

Aelred's beatitude is itself the subject of a vision to an unnamed monk, a vision revealing not Aelred's nearness to death, which everyone already knew, but the state of his soul. The brother who receives this vision sees Aelred lying as though in death, then in 'the form of a man shining with a brightness greater than that of the sun' (52). Another man 'of most pleasing countenance, dress and speech', surely an angel, explicates the vision to him, explaining that Aelred will not die until his soul is cleared entirely of reproach, when the last 'tiny cloud' is 'changed into light, and when it is he will go to God' (54).

Understanding what he has seen and heard as a promise of Aelred's immediate passage to beatitude, the monk is 'overcome by the newness of such great joy'. The truth of this vision is attested, says Walter, by the man's 'unstained life' and the knowledge that he is 'one worthy to see the truth even in his sleep, especially the truth about a father of such great sanctity' (54). Aelred's holiness of life has not only brought him prophetic visions of truth, but revealed itself to another similarly worthy.[87]

This experience, which sets Aelred spiritually apart from his monks and prepares him for his final departure, appropriately comes as he lies physically separated from the life of the community. Despite the constant visits of the monks to him and his intimate awareness of everything taking place in their lives, he is no longer a part of the life of the community, no longer in church for office, no longer in chapter each day. Seldom alone in body, he is nonetheless largely alone in spirit, and able at last to be alone with God. As he had written to the contemplative audience of *On the Institution of Recluses,* '[the recluse] must sit alone . . . believing that when alone she is never alone, for then she is with Christ, and he would not care to be with her in a crowd'.[88] Aelred, alone in heart and spirit, is at last alone with Christ.

Walter insists in this final portion of the *Vita* that while Aelred had been throughout his life a man of God, in his age and infirmity he became truly holy. The half of the work devoted to Aelred's final ten years tells of his illness, his dispensation from normal activity, his spiritual reading and writing, his patient days

[87]This vision recalls a similar one in Aelred's *The Nun of Watton,* by means of which a member of the community is assured of another sister's reception into beatitude: PL 195:790–91; CF 56.
[88]Inst incl 5; CCCM 1641; CF 2:50.

of conversation with the monks who came to sit and talk in his presence, his prayer and meditation, and his angelic visitations. His months of painful longing for the coming of Christ and finally his holy death and burial are the most memorable portions of the *Vita*, dominating it in length, in placement, and in clarity of organization and argument, so impressing the figure of the Aelred of those days upon the reader.

The inexorable movement of Walter's narrative toward sorrow at the abbot's death and joy at his release from pain and entry into beatitude culminates in the moment at which Aelred is identified with Christ in his final words: 'Into thy hands I commend my spirit' (61).[89] Finally, Walter writes of the transfiguration of his body in death, 'the glory . . . revealed in the father', in 'the beauty of one who sleeps' (62). His body washed, anointed, and carried into the church, Aelred is at last buried within the chapter-house; there ends the story Walter has to tell.

THE LETTER TO MAURICE

The Letter to Maurice is addressed to a certain 'lord Maurice', who had conveyed to Walter the objections to the *Vita* posed by two unnamed prelates. Powicke speculates that this figure may have been either the Maurice who was in 1167 prior of Kirkham, a community of Austin canons near Rievaulx also founded in 1132 by Walter Espec, or, less probably, Maurice of Rievaulx, Aelred's predecessor who had resigned after only two years as abbot.[90] Although Maurice of Rievaulx was probably dead by 1167, Maurice of Kirkham might well have been waiting for an opportunity to attack Aelred. Bad feeling between Kirkham and Rievaulx, with special animosity toward Aelred, went back to the 1140s when Waldef, Aelred's boyhood friend, left Kirkham, where he had been prior, to become a Cistercian. In 1148 he was elected

---

[89]See Heffernan, pp. 74–87.

[90]Powicke, pp. xxx–xxxi. Although this Maurice resigned his abbacy after only two years rather than leaving it by death, Walter's use of verbs in the past tense (*uidi et bene noui*) when writing of him in the *Vita* (33) seems to rule him out as the audience of the Letter to Maurice.

abbot at Melrose Abbey, a daughter of Rievaulx founded by David. As Waldef was thought by the canons at Kirkham to have been influenced in his decision by Aelred, it would not be surprising if the news of Aelred's death led to an outbreak of old resentment.[91] Maurice of Kirkham seems a likely candidate for the recipient of Walter's Letter.

Walter's defense of himself and his work to his critics is characteristically heated as he objects that they 'strive to becloud what I have done in the mists of uncertainty, and use the force of their authority to cast it into the pit of their suspicion and besmirch it as untrustworthy' (66). Yet the objections raised by the two prelates seem trivial when compared with conventional assertions of medieval hagiography. The *Vita*'s praise of Aelred is not particularly extravagant: Aelred's piety and charity seem unexceptionable, his miracles include only prayers for the stability of his monks, healings, and knowledge of his monks' wrongdoing, and Walter suggests no expectation that Aelred will continue to exercise power from beyond the grave. What in the *Vita* so offended these two men that they were prompted to attack Walter's account?

The stated issues, so far as one can tell from Walter's responses, were three: that Walter has failed to provide substantiation for Aelred's miracles, has misled his audience into believing Aelred to have been chaste as a youth, and has described Aelred's body in a way that was simply not credible.

To the claim that he has offered insufficient evidence Walter reacts with outrage, interpreting it as an implicit attack on his honesty. He complains that he has been 'branded as a liar' by the prelates and exclaims that 'it should have sufficed to clear me in the eyes of all men that in the course of the work I asserted that I had published nothing which I had not seen or heard, and that I had omitted very many fine things which I had confirmed by the verbal testimony of saintly monks' (66). He further protests that to 'insert the names of the witnesses upon whom [he] relied in the account of the miracles' (66) would be unconventional, 'Since

---

[91]Jocelin of Furness, p. 257; see Powicke, pp. lxxi-lxxv.

only a few authors have made use of this kind of statement in their description of Lives of the fathers and given the particular names of their sources'.[92]

Finally Walter turns the attack back upon his critics, claiming that their own viciousness keeps them from recognizing Aelred's virtue:

> whoever rejects what is true, if what is preached bears the stamp of truth, shows that he himself is darkness, and does not recognize the image of light when he hears it. For if he were light, he would recognize to be true what is part of the light, because like recognizes like, whereas the bad man defends the cause of the bad as his own. . . . How shameful, that prelates, heedless prelates, do not believe that the merits of a saint have given birth to miracles. . . . bad men scoff at the things done by the good. Hence it is not to be wondered at if men of this kind hesitate to put faith in the virtues of our father. (70)

Despite his anger, Walter accedes to the request that he substantiate the miracles, within the Letter itself naming witnesses, then adding four additional miracles from each of the four stages of Aelred's life—his infancy, childhood, young adulthood, and age—each buttressed with its own set of named witnesses. Walter thus not only insists on the accuracy of the *Vita* but advances new proofs of Aelred's sanctity and provides a few biographical details as well.

The first of the Letter's miracles, for example, shows Aelred to have been marked for sanctity while yet in the cradle and for the first time refers to members of Aelred's family. On a visit to Hexham, Walter says, William, son of Thole, later an archdeacon in the church of York, 'a kinsman of Aelred and very fond of the child's father and mother', saw the infant's face 'turned to the likeness of the sun', with his hand before him both reflecting his image and casting a shadow on the facing wall.[93] Recognizing in Aelred a 'new sun which had risen in the house', William told

---

[92]Powicke comments here that 'the practice of authenticating miracles by a list of witnesses was by no means new'; see p. 67, note.

[93]For more information on William son of Thole see Charles Clay, *Yorkshire Archaeological Journal*, 36 (1946): 284–5; see also Frank Barlow, *Durham Jurisdictional Peculiars* (Oxford, 1950) pp. 153–6.

the parents 'about the incomparable glory which he had seen in the child's face', revealing to them that their child would grow up to be 'a man of virtue' (71).

Walter's purpose in telling this story is, of course, to show Aelred as a new Moses, wreathed in infancy in the same brightness he would show in death. But as Walter gave no evidence of such infant holiness in Aelred in the *Vita*, his offering this story in response to the attack not only on his honesty but, implicitly, on Aelred's sanctity indicates his effort to recall some such incident with which to answer his and Aelred's critics.

The biographically intriguing part of this narrative is not the event—most parents have heard praise of their children from friends and relatives—but the statement authenticating it, with its identification of the members of Aelred's family present that day: 'When he was old enough to understand it, his father, his mother, his brothers told him about it, I heard it from his own lips, and others heard it from him' (71). The mention of Aelred's mother twice in this story is her only appearance in all that has been written by or about Aelred from that day to this. Walter's mention of Aelred's brothers, though, corroborates and comple-ments Richard of Hexham's identification of them in the *History of the Church of Hexham*.[94] It also suggests that they were older than Aelred, that he was the third of the three sons rather than, as might have been inferred from the special arrangements made for his upbringing, the eldest.

Walter's failure here to mention a sister for Aelred indicates that any daughters born to the family must have been younger than he, as none seems to have been present at the time of William son of Thole's visit. Walter's identification in the *Vita* of the audience of Aelred's *On the Institution of Recluses* as 'his sister, the chaste virgin who was a recluse' (41), along with Aelred's address to the audience of that work as his sister 'by birth and in spirit' and his insistence that they were 'begotten by the same father and borne within the same womb',[95] indicates that Eilaf's family included

---

[94]See note 17.
[95]Inst incl 1; CCCM 1:637; CF 2:43; Inst incl 32; CCCM 1:673–4; CF 2:93.

at least one daughter in addition to the three brothers. Walter's omission of her in this passage, apparently forgetting her existence, is curious.

The second of the miracles of the Letter again shows Aelred at home, telling his father of the as yet unreported death of the archbishop of York. While the story adds no new information about Aelred's family, mentioning none of its members except his father, Eilaf shows a wry personality recognizably like Aelred's in his description of Walter in *Spiritual Friendship* or his ancestral recollections in *The Saints of Hexham*. In response to Aelred's news, Walter says of Eilaf that: 'The man laughs to hear this, and all the family also, and commenting on Aelred's prophecy with whimsical politeness [*lepida urbanitate*] says, "True, my son, he is dead who lives an evil life."' This passage also verbally compares Eilaf with Our Lady and so Aelred with Jesus, perhaps suggesting that by this time his mother had died, leaving Eilaf to be father and mother at once: 'And his father, in the fulness of his joy, treasured the things said about him and pondered them in his heart' (72).

Walter's prelatial critics had objections beyond unsubstantiated miracles, however. They also rejected the reference to Aelred's having lived like a monk at court and the description of his dead body 'as glowing like a carbuncle and smelling like incense'. Walter treats this criticism as particularly frivolous, reporting that they chided him with having 'not expressed yourself with sufficient caution' (76). Walter does not attempt to restrain his fury at their combination of presumption, hostility, and willful stupidity. One is hard put not to sympathize with him. Not only are the criticisms petty, but they show, as Walter recognized, that his critics have not read the work carefully, seeming merely to have sought in it something they might reject.

Despite his anger, Walter replies, meanwhile almost accidentally again offering a new piece of new biographical information. First he explains his critics' complaint: 'It is that, because in that same period of his life Aelred occasionally deflowered his chastity I ought not to have compared a man of that sort to a monk.' His words were never intended to refer to chastity, he replies, but to humility:

When I applied the word monk to Aelred I was making use
of this figure, attributing a part by means of the whole, calling
him a monk not because he was completely chaste but because
he was truly humble. (76)

Walter's argument here is not specious, as it is sometimes
considered, but accurate. The passage in the *Vita* can only have
been misunderstood on purpose. Having praised the young Aelred
for his patience and prudence, peace and piety while acting 'as a
second lord and prince over a host of officials and all the men of
the court' (3), Walter had concluded: 'He was so fervent in spirit
that in the hall of kings he was looked upon rather as a monk than
as given to the service of the world and the display of office' (4).

While Walter had neglected in the *Vita* to mention Aelred's
early sexual experience, the words in question do not seem intended to allude to sexual purity, and the casualness with which
the Letter admits to Aelred's having lost his virginity before conversion suggests both that the fact was generally known, or perhaps
assumed, and that he saw no more need to deny it later than
to discuss it earlier. Aelred was not the first sexually experienced
person to have undergone conversion to monastic life as an adult.[96]
Walter's irritation with his critics here seems to have little to do
with the question of Aelred's sexual experience.

The prelates' other criticism seems equally trivial. As Walter
himself points out, his description of Aelred's body as beautiful and
aromatic in death was well established in saints' lives. Not content,
however, to answer his critics, he first attacks them, comparing
them to 'a peasant or an ignorant man' and judging them inferior
to a beast: 'Even a mole, though it has no eyes, shrinks in fear
from the ways of the sun. My blind friends do not blush to offend

[96]Jean Leclercq, *Monks and Love in Twelfth-Century France*, trans. R. R.
Bowker (1979; New York: Oxford University Press, 1987), notes that one result
of twelfth-century monastic orders' admission of adult postulants was the presence
of men with both military and sexual experience, with a consequent change
in the nature of the sermons and treatises written by and for such men. This
difference may be one of the reasons for the special devotion of cistercian writers
to the Song of Songs, as their own experience in the world allowed them to
find its language meaningful for writing about the love between Christ and the
Church or Christ and the soul.

against the light' (77). Having insisted on the traditional authority and present appropriateness of hyperbole (*superlatio*), Walter insists that in the case of Aelred's body he spoke the simple truth, despite having 'magnified the incomparable': 'Never before in life was that fair and seemly man habited in flesh so bright as when he lay in death. I say without a grain of falsehood that I never saw such bright flesh on any man, dead or alive.'[97]

The fact that these criticisms raised against the *Vita* so quickly after it appeared implies that the prelates had been lying in wait to attack Aelred as soon as he was no longer able to defend himself. The reasons for such an attack must not have been very pointed, however, as the two men seem to have frittered away their attack in questioning the truth of Aelred's miracles and challenging the accuracy of just two sentences from the *Vita*. Their expression of doubt about the beauty of Aelred's body in death seems a foolish rather than a serious attack on either Aelred or Walter. And while it is tempting to consider that their real interest lay in calling attention to Aelred's youthful sexual experience, the *Vita* contains no evidence for such an inference.

Heffernan has suggested that the prelates' real issue was with the center of Walter's argument, his claim of Aelred's sanctity, and that Walter recognized it as such: 'He viewed it as an attack which impugned the accuracy of the entire life. . . . [and] raised the issue of Aelred's sanctity; to doubt the presence of the miraculous in Aelred's life implied, for Walter, a suspicion of his sanctity.'[98]

The unfocused criticisms of the prelates seem finally to have arisen largely from a simple dislike of Aelred and a consequent desire to debunk anything said or written about him and so to resist any formal attempt to celebrate his life. It seems likely that the anxiety of Abbot H and Walter Daniel to have a Life written and available to the monastic world as quickly after Aelred's death as possible was due to their awareness of the readiness of Maurice

[97]Heffernan, pp. 120–22, notes that this passage also consciously echoes the gospel descriptions of Christ in the Transfiguration, as well as various apocalyptic passages.
[98]Heffernan, p. 106.

and the other prelates to attack Aelred as soon as he was safely out of hearing. No figure as active and widely known in the world as Aelred had been until the last months of his life could have lacked opponents, and those who hated or even feared him may well have been eager to resist any continuation of his authority or citation of his moral power.

Moreover, if what had angered the complaining prelates was Aelred's public acclaim and influence during his life, Walter's care to portray him almost entirely as a private man, a monk, an abbot, and a spiritual father must have left them frustrated, finding little to criticize in the *Vita* and so driven to trivialities: miracles without named witnesses and two encomiastic sentences that seemed 'insufficiently careful' to them. The fact that those who moved quickly to criticize the *Vita* seem not to have read it carefully is further evidence that they had no particular object except objecting; Walter's outrage at being called to defend his unexceptionable eulogy for his abbot seems altogether justified.

Indeed the passion with which Walter defends his work and his abbot, already familiar from the *Vita*, becomes in the course of the Letter almost a theme in itself. He begins by assuring Maurice that he intends brevity—'I am not going to wander into prolixity'— but immediately qualifies the promise, explaining that 'the two prelates who . . . use the force of their authority to cast [the *Vita*] into the pit of their suspicion and besmirch it as untrustworthy, compel me to write at some length' (66). Toward the end of the work he recalls his intention to be concise, 'lest the prolixity of this letter should put too hard a strain on your attention and this long-drawn conclusion be burdensome in your ears' (77). Meanwhile he attacks the virtue, literacy, and intelligence of his critics, refers to them sarcastically as 'my two friends who in their simplicity have thought fit to rebuke me' (75), addresses them as 'Oh, you dullards!' (77), and scorns their purposes and understandings from first to last. The Letter is a window into the mind and heart of Walter.

What drove these men, and how great a role the anticipation of their attacks played in urging Abbot H and Walter to write the

Vita Aelredi, is unknown. But it is thanks to them that the Letter to Maurice exists, with its few but valuable contributions to the history of Aelred.

Walter concludes the Letter with one more narrative insisting on Aelred's sanctity as revealed above all in his charity. This story, while not miraculous, is surely an instance of Aelred's superhuman patience, humility, and charity in the midst of suffering, an incident that allows Walter himself for a moment to emerge from the shadows into full participation. Once as he sat alone with Aelred in his hut, he says, a monk 'mad with rage, . . . a bovine creature of criminal aspect, moving in the vilest disorder' appeared; finding Aelred crouching on a mat beside the hearth 'rubbing his painful limbs . . . looking by the fire like a leaf of parchment', he lifted the mat and 'hurled the father of at least a hundred monks and five hundred laymen into the fire among the cinders.' Walter says nothing about rescuing Aelred from the fire, but reports his furious retaliation:

> I was consumed by the sight, and not suffering the danger to the father, rose in hot indignation against the bully . . . and took him hard by the beard. The giant . . . hurled his great hulking body upon me, but my spirit was roused and I withstood him bodily and checked his malicious efforts.

By this time other monks had appeared to join in the attack on 'the son of pestilence', but Aelred, 'mindful only of the call of charity', called them back, assured them that he was unhurt, and then 'taking [the attacker's] head in his hands, the most blessed man kisses him, blesses and embraces him, and gently sought to soothe his senseless anger against himself' (80).

With this story Walter ends the Letter, concluding with renewed praise of Aelred's 'perfect charity . . . which, though so grievously exasperated by an inferior, renders no account, but on the contrary repays mad folly with kindness, surely the most perfect pledge of love.' He calls finally on Maurice to read this story to the two prelates 'that they may know that the miracles wrought by Aelred, who brought forth such fruits in his charity, were grounded in his merits' (81).

THE PURPOSE OF THE *VITA AELREDI*

What kind of work is the *Vita,* and why did Walter Daniel write it? The answer appears obvious: its insistence on Aelred's 'outshining sanctity' and its dependence on hagiographical models define it as a saint's life. And the conventions that shape the work are also hagiographical.[99]

But as Walter sought to present Aelred as a man of God, set apart by his virtue and his love of God and neighbor, he wrote neither to create a cult around Aelred nor to initiate canonization proceedings for him. His stated goal was the preservation of Aelred's memory for those who already knew and loved him and for those who would otherwise not know him at all. The immediate cause of his writing, however, seems to have been a desire to ward off anticipated criticism of Aelred. By insisting on his humility and charity, Walter endeavored to refute charges that he was proud, ambitious, and overly involved in the affairs of the world rather than devoted to the needs of his community and the cistercian life of contemplation. The *Vita* is thus also an apology, designed to preserve the memory of Aelred as an attentive abbot, who loved and wept over his spiritual sons 'as a mother' while bringing economic prosperity and intensity of religious life to two different abbeys, and as a spiritual man through whom God saved and healed.

Walter writes for the world in which Aelred is already known and loved. He begins by speaking of Aelred to Abbot H as a loved father and friend to them both and ends with Aelred's being laid to rest beside Abbot William, known at least by report to both Walter and Abbot H. The work includes no miracles done by Aelred in childhood or after death, suggests no great temptation of or spiritual struggle by Aelred in his youth or adulthood, and makes no claim that Aelred will exercise care or protection for those who remember him or that his body will remain incorrupt

[99]Powicke, p. lxxvi: 'The *Vita Ailredi* was written to prove Ailred's claim to sanctity. It is a piece of hagiography.'

in death.[100] It concludes not by declaring Aelred's sanctity, but rather by promising that he will benefit in death from the holiness of Abbot William:

> He was taken for burial in the chapter-house next to his predecessor, the venerable, saintly and first abbot of Rievaulx, William, whom we have mentioned above, and with whom and for whose merits and the grace of the Saviour seen in him he will rejoice and be glad exceedingly, as is right, before God and Our Lord Jesus Christ, to whom be the glory for ever and ever. Amen. (64)

Far from commending Aelred in his sanctity to Alexander III, who would probably have remembered the value of Aelred's support for his papal claim only fifteen years earlier, Walter allows Aelred to rest in body and in hope with Abbot William.

In his prefatory letter to the *Vita* Walter states his goal to celebrate Aelred's life and preserve his memory, 'flooding with its brightness the memory of generations to come' (1). At the end of the letter Walter returns to this theme, now adding his intent to provide a record of Aelred's life as a pattern for others (2).

Walter has two additional purposes in writing. Although he is guided by his own love for and veneration of his dead abbot, he is also immediately concerned to satisfy a previous request from Abbot H: 'Our father's recent death is as strong an enforcement of your wish: it drives us forward, orders obedience, enjoins fulfillment of your instructions' (1). As Walter acknowledges the request and reports Aelred's death in almost the same breath, he must already have written most of the *Vita* during the final months of Aelred's life. He probably wrote the letter last rather than first. Had he written the letter before the *Vita*, by the time he finished there would have been no reason to announce Aelred's death. And the hypothesis that he was already at work while Aelred still lived explains the *Vita*'s disproportionate attention to his last four years.

Walter presents his third reason for writing indirectly, perhaps even inadvertently, unable to distinguish his own concerns from

---

[100]See Donald Weinstein and Rudolph M. Bell, *Saints and Society* (Chicago: University of Chicago Press, 1982), for a discussion of the conventional marks of sanctity in medieval saints' lives, esp. pp. 102–20.

the story he tells. He may not have intended to mention his anxiety
about imminent challenge, but his references to the difficulty he
foresees in fulfilling Abbot H's instructions and his allusions to
those who will doubt him indicate his concern to refute already
current accusations against Aelred.

> I long to do more than I can, and my will is to hold fast
> to the truth. May your fatherly prayers be with me and the
> devotions of your sons uphold me in my task and make the
> truth to prevail over the opinion of many—the truth, that is, of
> such a life and character as may astonish many good men, who,
> however meritorious, find it hard to admit the truth. (1)

While this appeal may be prompted merely by an anticipation
of difficulty in recording Aelred's sanctity, Walter's concern with
'the opinion of many' and an echoing phrase a few lines later
defining the work's intended audience as those 'who are willing
to see' (2) suggest that the opinion of at least some was already
becoming a problem to Aelred's friends. It may well have been
awareness of these critics that prompted Abbot H to ask Walter,
apparently the most prolific writer at Rievaulx other than Aelred
himself, to compose a summary of Aelred's life as a monk by which
to show Aelred's humility and spiritual gifts and thereby answer
accusations of pride and ambition. Just such anxiety for Aelred's
reputation must underlie Walter's lengthy defense of Aelred's enthusiastic acquisition of land for Revesby, as well as his apparently
gratuitous report and rejection of the rumor of Aelred's ambition
and self-indulgence at the time of his election to the abbacy of
Rievaulx.

The charges that prompted Walter to write seem to have
been directed toward Aelred's public life. The *Vita*'s emphasis on
Aelred's love for his monks and the affection and respect in which
they held Aelred as their spiritual father indicates that the rumors
about him, 'the opinion of many' that Walter sought to refute,
concerned not his personal relationships but his activity in the
world outside the cloister, his pleasure in the company of the rich
and powerful of the realm. Although accusations that he was self-
indulgent—'a glutton and a wine-bibber and a friend of publicans'
(34)—are also on Walter's mind as he writes, he hints at no more

pointed personal attacks, no suppositions about Aelred's character
and personal life. Aelred receives praise rather than criticism for
the warmth with which he turned the jealous knight at court from
an enemy to a friend, the patient care he expended on the unstable
monk, the gracious healing of the young man who had swallowed
a frog, and the tender and uncritical welcome with which in his
final years he received his monks around his bed.

But whereas Walter writes freely and apparently openly about
such personal interactions, he consciously ignores Aelred's public
life and excuses what he cannot ignore. He says enough that
no one can accuse him of hiding the truth, while consistently
underplaying those aspects of Aelred's career, enveloping them
within reports of miracles and lengthy discussions of Aelred's piety
and humility. He writes little of Aelred's trips away from home,
essentially ignores his interaction with Henry II, and fails to mention the works he wrote for presentation outside the monastery.

The attacks on Aelred that quickly appeared under cover of
criticism of the *Vita* offer additional evidence that it was written to
defend Aelred and protect his reputation. The objections that met
the work and Walter's consequent angry determination to stand by
it resulted in an even more forceful argument for Aelred's sanctity
in the Letter to Maurice. Thus the Letter not only indicates
the existence of opposition to Aelred at the time of his death
and explains the rapidity with which Walter produced the *Vita*,
but strengthens the case that Aelred's opponents had sought to
weaken. It is no wonder that awareness of a local faction hostile
to Aelred should have prompted Abbot H and Walter to preserve
his memory in terms chosen by them rather than by his detractors.
The prefatory letter's implication that the work was already almost
completed when Aelred died suggests that Aelred's friends knew
the importance of getting their point of view out quickly, before
the opposition was able to strike.

While the *Vita Aelredi* was written to show Aelred's sanctity
to a local audience made up mostly of those who knew, revered,
and loved the abbot of Rievaulx, people like Gilbert of Hoyland
and Reginald of Durham, its audience also included some who
knew, or at least knew of, Aelred, and did not like what they

knew. Whether they were jealous of the esteem in which others held him, like the knight from Aelred's youth, or resentful of occasions on which he had decided some dispute against them, like the angry visiting abbot, they were ready to blame, even eager to go on the attack, now that the cowardice that had held them silent during Aelred's life was no longer necessary.

And while Walter surely wrote to preserve the memory of the great abbot and to offer his life as a model, he also wrote to reject these people's accusations. If during Aelred's life some had opposed him, spread rumors about him, attacked him verbally, and even thrown him bodily into the fire, in his death they and others like them were sure to continue their attacks. It seems probable that Walter's rage when he writes of the jealous monk and the vituperative visiting abbot, whom he describes as 'much too inclined to contumely and . . . cunningly ill-natured' (44), was directed not so much at those figures, by the time of his writing already dead, but at those others whose hostility still threatened Aelred's memory.

THE BIOGRAPHICAL QUESTION

It is inevitable that the *Vita* and the Letter to Maurice should be employed as sources for biographies of Aelred: they are by far the most complete documents extant for his life and character. The two works, however, are in no sense modern biographies, and to treat them as such or even as reliable sources is to misrepresent them and, on that basis, to produce fundamentally flawed studies of Aelred's life.[101] For rather than endeavoring to report the events, both private and public, in the life of Aelred in order to construct

---

[101]As an example of the risk of misunderstanding the difference between the work shaped by hagiographical convention and that dependent on documentary sources, see John Ayto and Alexandra Barratt, ed., *Aelred of Rievaulx's De Institutione Inclusarum*, EETS o.s. 287 (London: Oxford University Press, 1984) p. xi. Their claim that the *Vita* 'is not free from some of the usual exaggerations of the hagiographer, [but] is by and large a reliable work' is either tautological or unverifiable. That is, as a saint's life it is reliable insofar as it is a saint's life, but finally the judge of Walter's accuracy in arguing Aelred's sanctity can only be God. Ayto and Barratt presumably intend their statement, however, as an evaluation of the *Vita's* reliability as a source for modern biography. In the

a historically accurate representation, Walter concentrates on him as a patient and loving monk and abbot, a healer and teacher and visionary. His Aelred reveals God's power through his prayers and miracles. In holiness of mind and spirit he is less an historical figure from twelfth-century Yorkshire than a representative man of God, more like the blessed saints than distinct from them in human individuality.[102]

Walter seeks to reveal Aelred's sanctity through his actions, rather than exploring those acts as though they had inherent meaning, as modern biographers would do. The *Vita* is thus incomplete and even inaccurate in reporting the details of his life. It provides no information about his experience before entering David's court and next to none about his public life after his conversion. It says nothing of his friendships and names only about half his works.

Walter's decision to concentrate on Aelred as monk and abbot means that he provides little information about Aelred's life outside the monastery, and his desire to emphasize Aelred's humility and charity means that he says little of Aelred's acquaintance with the great and powerful. The portrait he creates is partial, incomplete, flat rather than developed. It offers valuable insights about Aelred's life and personality, but it has too many flaws to stand alone even as a portrait. The *Vita* includes the bare outlines of Aelred's vocational career: the years at the court of David and his role there, his conversion and entrance into monastic life, his journey to Rome for Abbot William, and his time as novice master and then abbot at Revesby and Rievaulx. It says little of what Aelred was actually doing during those years, nothing about trips to Clairvaux or the General Chapter at Cîteaux and nothing about visitations to daughter houses. Although in Walter's account the dying Aelred recalls that he frequently left Rievaulx for visits to court, his historical works indicate that he was in demand as a guest preacher, and Reginald of Durham reports that he was a

---

absence of documentary evidence for most of what Walter includes it is difficult to know how they reached their conclusion.

[102]See Heffernan, pp. 14, 20.

friend of and visitor to the hermit Godric of Finchale, Walter ignores those aspects of Aelred's life.

Walter's decision to concentrate on the sanctity of Aelred as monk and abbot also causes him to be silent even about the demands that reached from the outside world into the monastery. In representations of monastic life and of himself as teacher and abbot in the dialogues of *The Mirror of Charity, On the Soul,* and *Spiritual Friendship,* Aelred repeatedly uses visitors to the abbey as structural devices to begin or interrupt the abbot's conversations with his monks, thus revealing his concern about their interference with his responsibility to community life. At the beginning of *On the Soul,* for example, when a brother asks the fictional Aelred to explain something from 'the works of Saint Augustine', his response is 'I am at your service. For now that these people have finished the business for which they came, they have departed.'[103] Yet Walter mentions only one such visitor, the contumacious abbot.

The inaccuracies in the work are perhaps more distracting; what Walter does not say remains merely a mystery, but what he reports incorrectly will lead all but the most cautious into certain error. His chronological reconstruction of various periods in Aelred's life violates dates ascertainable from other sources, his summaries of Aelred's works sometimes conflict with the works themselves, and he sometimes in the Letter reconsiders and withdraws statements made in the *Vita.* In chapters 37 through 39, for example, he presents a series of events involving a chronology that cannot be correct. He says that after the death of an abbot, which probably took place in 1166, Aelred paid a visit to Galloway and returned to Rievaulx four years before his death, which occurred in 1167.[104]

Again, the statement that Aelred as abbot of Revesby was 'greatly beloved . . . by the whole realm and most of all by the king' (29) must surely project Aelred's relationship with Henry II back into the years when Aelred was young and Stephen was king. The summary of *On the Institution of Recluses* that says that Aelred

[103]Anima 1.1; CCCM 1:683; CF 22:35.
[104]See Powicke, p. 45 n. 1.

'traced the course of this kind of profession from the ardour of the entrance into the same to its perfection' (41) is simply incorrect, apparently based on at best rough familiarity with the beginning and, perhaps, the end of the work. The Letter both forgets Aelred's sister, 'the chaste virgin who was a recluse' (41), and timidly retracts the claim that Aelred's curse killed the angry abbot (68).

The *Vita*'s combination of incompleteness and inaccuracy arises not only from Walter's emphasis on Aelred's charity, humility, and piety, but also from his reliance on his own experience during his years of familiarity with Aelred as his primary source. Hence his work preserves the ailing and humble monk and abbot and eliminates the man of the world beyond the cloister. The *Vita* has little to say about the years before 1150, when Walter entered Rievaulx, but focuses on Aelred's last years, when Walter was, presumably, his scribe and *medicus*. Walter's real subject is the years during which Aelred was at home, increasingly frail and bedridden, relieved of abbatial duties and unable to travel because of illness. During those years he was available to listen and give spiritual counsel to Walter and others. Walter portrays him as elderly and suffering, gentle, patient, increasingly dependent on others' care of him, and freed from the demands of travel and administration for reading, writing, and contemplation. It is this man who receives 'visitations of divine grace and angelic conversations' (50) and 'the spirit of prophecy' (51) and appears in a vision to a fellow monk, 'shining with a brightness greater than that of the sun' (52).

This Aelred lives on in the minds and hearts of the *Vita*'s readers: a sensitive abbot who spends his days listening to those in need and offering them spiritual guidance through his spoken and written words. As Aelred's love and concern for his monks made itself known in all he did, Walter says, he tolerated things that many other abbots would have punished: 'He did not treat them with the pedantic imbecility habitual in some silly abbots who, if a monk takes a brother's hand in his own, or says anything that they do not like, demand his cowl, strip and expel him' (40).

Walter not only portrays primarily the elderly Aelred, but his own view of sanctity colors the portrait. As Walter writes to record

Aelred's humility and piety and to reject charges that Aelred was too often outside the monastery or that he was ambitious and overly involved in public life, the man he portrays is inevitably not the traveler and advisor of kings, but the frail father of spiritual sons, who sought to create at Rievaulx a place that 'above all else . . . teaches tolerance of the infirm and compassion with others in their necessities' (37). Walter's Aelred is the abbot who wept over monks who sought to leave and held the dying in his arms (36).

There seems no reason to doubt the accuracy of this portrait, whose truth is borne out by the voices of such contemporary figures as Gilbert of Hoyland and Jocelin of Furness and by Aelred's own sermons and works of spiritual guidance. It is nonetheless incomplete, offering no glimpse of the public figure and the friend of the great, in demand as witness, counselor, and speaker, and entirely neglecting the brilliant, acerbic, and witty man who appears in his own works. Walter's description of *On the Institution of Recluses,* for example, not only summarizes the work inaccurately but fails to suggest its pointed depictions of the old women who gather around anchoresses' cells to share gossip and its warnings against the romantic yearnings gentle words may create even in those vowed to virginity.

The verbal caricaturist who with a few strokes in *Spiritual Friendship* visually records the irascible Walter is absent from the *Vita,* as are the moral historian who records his perspective on the significance of the Battle of the Standard, the humanist who experiments with ciceronian dialogue, and the popular preacher and raconteur who includes in his homily *On the Saints of Hexham* stories of his ancestors' efforts to take just a few small bones of the saints for their own purposes. All these public faces of Aelred are absent from the *Vita.* The Aelred whom Gilbert of Hoyland remembered as a man of wit and passion, 'endued with a ready understanding but a passionate affection',[105] is all but invisible in Walter's portrayal of a gentle, sensitive, humble abbot.

[105]SC 40.6 [PL 41.6]; PL 184:218; CF 26:497.

For while Walter records and celebrates Aelred's contemplative holiness and the love in which the community held their abbot, he omits much of the larger reality of Aelred's life and sanctity, striving to make his case by rejecting those portions of his abbot's life and personality that do not accord with his own understanding of human holiness, or perhaps with the understanding of his age. Believing passionately that Aelred was a man of God, he does not mention those aspects of Aelred's life that he thinks might distract others from that truth or persuade them to deny it.

No wonder then that the Aelred who lives in modern minds is a frail, passive figure whose charity appears consistently in humility and patience rather than in the outgoing assertiveness of his early years. The aged abbot lying on his bed as others gather around to talk endures in memory because it was he whom Walter knew best, he whom Walter wished to present so as to ward off the trouble he saw ahead.

Walter's struggle with the shape and meaning of Aelred's life and his understanding of human holiness as primarily a thing of the spirit, manifested through miracles, prayer, visions, and endurance in charity, are responsible for the compelling portrait he left of Aelred. He achieved that portrait, however, at the expense of the wholeness of the man he portrays. Had he been able to see in Aelred's public life the love for the world palpable in Aelred's own works and to recognize that love as also an expression of Aelred's sanctity, he might have painted a portrait that offered more of the stuff of historical biography than is to be found in the *Vita* or the Letter to Maurice.

Treating the *Vita* as biography raises another difficulty. Readers may believe that the same evidence can satisfy two different purposes: to give both verifiable historical detail about the life of Aelred, son of Eilaf, and reliable insight into the spiritual reality of Aelred the saintly abbot. But those two purposes are not the same. They emerge from different understandings of human reality and the evidence proper to it. The biographer seeks information with which to reconstruct history so complete in its documentary grounding that its conclusions may be verified; the worshiper, who looks to see God at work in human life, must look beyond that which can be recorded in documents, knowing that truth lies not

in the place of birth or numbers of charters witnessed, but in the
relationship of the human spirit with God, a reality that must be
seen with the eye of faith.

Those who would reconstruct history or write biography
are required to doubt, to analyze, to 'unloose' the structure and
logic of their texts: they may not treat the sacred biography as
unchallengeable in its truth, but must hesitate before the author's
assertions and look for corroborative evidence outside the text.
Those who seek to know the the saint's spiritual reality must take
as true the witness and interpretation of the author who reports
it, as there is no other evidence available. They cannot challenge
the truth of the report they read but must accept that report itself
as conveying truth.

Heffernan explains this effect of the sacred biography by claiming that the work may come to participate in the meaning of the
sacred life it recounts. It becomes itself iconic, a relic, spiritualized;
the spiritual status of its subject is transferred to it:

> Sacred biography is not sacred scripture. However, if they both
> partake of inspiration, then we ought to consider that Au-
> gustine's remarks that 'these words were not written by hu-
> man industry, but were poured forth by divine intelligence'
> were undoubtedly believed to apply to these texts as well as to
> Scripture.[106]

Treating such a work as though it were biography is particularly tempting and particularly dangerous: the established tradition
of the work's truth makes it seem biographically reliable, but
its status as definitive, in its essence true, means that it is no
longer accessible to analysis and evaluation in relationship to other
documentary evidence and logic, but must be regarded as assured
reality. Rigorous biographical analysis may then offend those who
believe in the text as true, but a report built on unquestioning
trust moves one no closer to biography.

While readers of the *Vita Aelredi* are thus expected to take it on
its own terms, trusting Walter's witness to Aelred's sanctity, they
must remember that as its purpose is not to preserve the memory
of Aelred's life for its own sake or that of future historians but 'to

[106]Heffernan, p. 36.

reflect honor and glory to God',[107] that purpose has determined not only the detail Walter chooses to report but his interpretation of that detail. Further, those who accept the spiritual authority of the work must recognize that as it is not intended to be biography, biographers may reject some of its assertions and offer other ways of understanding the events of Aelred's life. All must thus remain cautious about seeking in the *Vita Aelredi* a truth beyond that which it claims.

CONCLUSION

Aelred of Rievaulx has been known through the centuries most fully by his own writings. There his combination of intellect and grace, wit and compassion, love of God and love of the world blend and pour forth, as Gilbert of Hoyland says, 'in the passion of inebriating grace'.[108] But because of the direction of the unknown Abbot H and the energy and devotion of Walter Daniel, Aelred's scribe, doctor, and friend, the Aelred who wrote those works lives on as a humble, patient sufferer, a contemplative seeker of God, a gentle father and spiritual guide to the monks of Rievaulx, and a gifted abbot who in twenty years turned a small young foundation into a thriving and compassionate community where the 'despised and rejected . . . [found] a place of rest' (37).

In the *Vita Aelredi* Walter carried out Abbot H's instructions. He so commemorated the father as to allow his life to 'flood with its brightness the memory of generations to come' (1), and he portrayed a man who from infancy until death shone with the light of God's glory. Resisting the charges of ambition and worldly involvement that apparently plagued Aelred's abbacy, Walter shows a very different abbot of Rievaulx. As in youth he chastised his body within his cell and in maturity prayed for the wandering, so in age he receives heavenly visions and engages in heavenly discourse. His physical agony allows him the more powerfully to guide and love his monks, not only answering their questions as the

[107]Heffernan, p. 35.
[108]SC 40 [PL 41.7]; PL 184:218; CF 26:497.

embers of his life fail, but showing charity even to the monk who throws him into the fire that warms against his body's chill (78-80).

It is ironic that in defending Aelred against his critics Walter implicitly accepts their standards. Rather than arguing—as Aelred could have done—that service to God's people, wherever they live, is service to God and that on this side of beatitude the *vita contemplativa* and the *vita activa* are inevitably joined, he yields the point. He restricts Aelred's life to the contemplative and monastic while ignoring his activity, his fascination with history past and in the making.

Despite twelfth-century cistercian anxiety about the propriety of an abbot's playing a role in the larger world, serving as political advisor to the king, writing works of historical guidance, and absenting himself from his community in order to preach and advise elsewhere, the cistercian abbots best remembered today are those who did just those things: Bernard of Clairvaux, Baldwin of Ford, and Aelred of Rievaulx. It is no wonder that David Knowles called Aelred the Bernard of the North: both of these great twelfth-century Cistercians found themselves torn between the contemplative silence they had left the world to find and the world whose needs called them relentlessly back.

As Bernard longed for the peace of the cloister and the vision of the face of God while chastising Eleanor of Aquitaine, challenging Peter Abelard, and preaching the Third Crusade, as Eugene III from the tumult of Rome remembered the woods and stones of Clairvaux, as Archbishop Baldwin looked back from the political struggles of Canterbury to the sunlit stretches of Ford, so Aelred in his turn, while traveling to Westminster or Watton or Galloway, must often have felt the tug of his community at Rievaulx, 'the church crowded with the brethren like bees in a hive . . . compacted into one angelical body' (38), 'that multitude of brethren [among whom] I found no one whom I did not love.'[109] He must have missed the place as well as the people, the crown of the high hills around the valley, the sweet sound and

[109]Spir amic 3.82; CCCM 1:334; CF 5:112.

'delicious melody' of the streams tumbling down, and the bell summoning the community to prayer.

Aelred himself best provides the impulse that brings together the two worlds that Walter Daniel views as irreconcilable and struggles to keep apart. Aelred recognized and wrote of the essential unity of human men and women with one another and with God, and he insisted that the monk in his cloister, the anchoress in her cell, and the king and queen on their thrones were all part of one world, God's world, and were mutually responsible for one another, called so long as this world endures to love both God and neighbor, so that in eternity all may be joined in unbroken friendship. In a sermon for the Ascension of the Virgin he writes:

> You see, if Mary had been alone in the house, no one would have fed the Lord; if Martha had been alone, no one would have tasted his presence and his words. . . . Do not neglect Mary for Martha, or Martha for Mary. If you neglect Martha, who will serve Jesus? And if you neglect Mary, what will be the use of Jesus' visit, since you will not taste his sweetness? Know, my brothers, that in this life it is necessary never to separate these two women. When the time comes that Jesus is no longer poor, no longer hungry or thirsty, no longer tempted, then only Mary, the spiritual action, will occupy the whole house: the dwelling of your soul.[110]

In the life of Aelred, monk and abbot, Mary and Martha lived always together in unity. In prayer, reading, and contemplation Aelred chose Mary's part, seeking wisdom and understanding, the sweetness of Jesus, to sustain his spirit for his journeys in the exercise of Martha's part: writing, preaching, building, healing, and counselling. Active in two worlds, loving those resident in both, and endeavoring to balance his responsibilities to God and to all sorts and conditions of humankind, Aelred lived one integrated and simple life of humility and charity, love of God and love of neighbor, always both tasting and offering up such food of the spirit that in him all may taste and see how sweet is the Lord.

Marsha L. Dutton

Hanover College

---

[110]S. 19.18, 21–2, 'In assumptione sanctae mariae', CCCM 1A:151.

THE LIFE OF AELRED

TO ABBOT H,[1] dearest of men, his servant W. Daniel, greeting. Our father is dead; he has vanished from our world like the morning sunshine, and many hearts long that this great light should flood with its brightness the memory of generations to come, and indeed of those still living for whom it shone in all its splendor. I cannot withhold from you, to whose bidding I owe all possible respect, what I know and feel at such a time; I am bound by a loving injunction which cannot be disregarded without vexation of spirit: 'to obey is better than sacrifice and to hearken than the fat of rams'.[2] Our father's recent death is as strong an enforcement of your wish: it drives us forward, orders obedience, enjoins fulfillment of your instructions. And yet, wretch that I am, what shall I do in the quandary in which I find myself? It strains my power and constrains my desire and blunts my will, for I long to do more than I can, and my will is to hold fast to the truth. May your fatherly prayers be with me and the devotions of your sons uphold me in my task and make the truth to prevail over the opinion of many—the truth, that is, of such a life and character as may astonish many good men, who, however meritorious, find it hard to admit the truth. For who would not hesitate to credit the charity and astonishing sanctity of the pure life of so great a father? But I must not in a preface try to exhaust

the limpid and abundant spring, lest, God forbid, the vessels of my
hearers fail before the waters have began to pour from the rock to
the refreshment alike of those now living and of future generations,
to whom the truth is apparent and falsehood can afford no pleasure. That they may know that I write the truth and avoid all else,
I call on him who made heaven and earth to be my witness that it
is quite beyond my power to set out the merits of him of whom I
long to speak as the facts appear to me. So far by way of prologue,
or, if you prefer, in the tenor of a letter. Now I proceed to dig
into noble ground and reveal the root of such great goodness, that
they who are willing to see may see the outshining sanctity of him
who begot me to the life of Saint Benedict through the Gospel of
God and showed himself a father to the brethren, and that his great
glory may not be hid in the earth and be concealed from those
who, thirsting in spirit, are wont to embrace examples of the good.

CHAPTER TWO. AELRED'S YOUTH

Our father was in boyhood remarkable, and even when of
tender years had the makings of a fine man, save that he had greater
virtue, and the vices of manhood were not possible in him. Young
men, however wise, sometimes can scarcely restrain their lust and
are swollen with pride, but he, in the time of adolescence, mindful
of the good things which he later found, began to meditate on
God and to perfect his holy meditations with works before he
had entered on his manhood.[3] As a boy, he was in the service of
the King of Scotland, that great, that second David; he was in the
world, like good fruit of the true vine, but in thought and will, he
was in heaven. Child though he was, he desired no worldly service,
but he was willing for a while and in some measure to serve a lord
so pure and holy, a man whose life inspired a veneration due to it,
a king whose authority gave strength to it. He had great humility,
and he was loath to leave the wise prince, so compassionate in the
exercise of his power, so chaste in the maintenance of his honor,
an example to him of constancy through steadfastness in what is
good, and the avoidance through bodily integrity of the pressures
of evil desire, fulfilling that precept of the first David, *Depart from*

evil and do good.[4] And, an even better and more profitable reason for this earthly service, he shared the rule of a great king and acquired from the best of leaders the royal virtues which later he was to describe in writing for the consolation of the faithful, and himself found profit in the reading of this consolation, and so did not merely make others bear fruit but himself bore fruit of sweet savour. As we shall explain later, in due course he wrote a most enlightening life of the aforesaid king.[5]

The king was so fond of him that he made him great in his house and glorious in his palace. He was put in charge of many things and was as a second lord and prince over a host of officials and all the men of the court, going in and out by the king's command, faithful in all things, friendly and welcome to the good, fearful and stern, though sympathetic, to the evil. For even then he observed the command 'love your enemies,' and was heedful of the saying 'I am made all things to all men that I might save them.'[6] Whence the king loved him exceedingly and every day was more and more considering how to advance him, so much so, indeed, that if he had not unexpectedly entered the Cistercian Order he would have honored him with the first bishopric of the land. In any case, he was steward[7] of the royal household. Nothing, inside or out, was done without him. He was respected by all in all things and never failed; and no wonder, for God had taught him patience and had enriched his active spirit with no little prudence, so that in the largeness of his pure heart he was without hatred or rancor, nourished no discord, no bitterness, and, though in a position to harm many, was serviceable to all. 0 man more precious than the fine gold of Ophir[8] and the topaz stone, who, even while in the garb of the world, could say with the Apostle, 'By the grace of God I am what I am: and his grace in me was not in vain,[9] for he was so fervent in spirit that in the hall[10] of kings he was looked upon rather as a monk[11] than as given to the service of the world and the display of office. Everything done at court was in his keeping, yet he did whatever he did with such mildness that under his just and affable management of affairs there was no unrest, no disturbance among the people. He set the foot of justice and walked in the paths of peace where truth could suffer no violence, and kept his inward eye fixed where he could the more sweetly and steadily see God. Often when, as the man in charge—for he was chief steward of the royal table—he stood in the presence of the king at dinner, serving the dishes and dividing the food in turn to the eaters, his thoughts would be in the other world, and oblivious to outward things, as one caught up in an ecstasy to the heavenly heights, he would forget the affairs of the belly in a pleasant excess of contemplation on the apostolic words: 'Meats for the belly, and the belly for meats: but God shall destroy both it and them.'[12] For he practiced from his boyhood spareness of living. In his dress he eschewed all superfluity, vainglory and wantonness, turning his vesture into a symbol and forecast of the admirable poverty of his later life. He avoided elaborate confections, as the wear of the proud and effeminate; his dress consisted of an ordinary toga and a cloak, each as simply and sparely cut as was consistent with decency. His graciousness and good will were so great that injury did not stir him up to anger, nor slander provoke him to vengeance; nor, through the grace of God, did contumely sting him to retaliation; so that he did even greater service to his enemies than to his friends, for his natural kindness disarmed ingratitude and the serenity of his own peaceable heart lit up, in contrast, the disordered mind of the ill-wisher. Throughout his life he took pains to return love for hate, good for evil, kindness for envy, the gracious word and the friendly deed for the ill-speaking. At this very time his marvelous patience was made known to all by another's malice, and was waited like a sweet smell from a rose pricked by a thorn.

CHAPTER 3. THE SCURRILOUS KNIGHT

There was a certain hard, stiff dolt of a fellow, quite intractable, a military man, at least in name, and certainly strong and cruel enough in the pursuit of evil. He had a mad hostility to the young man, because he enjoyed the king's special affection and was so popular with everybody in the palace. In his rage and envy he could not endure the sight of our Joseph and the gracious qualities which made him cherished as a father by the other knights, and honored and given the first place by acclamation both in general and private esteem. So he began to pursue him and in his hatred to molest him. He tried secretly to excite feelings of indignation against him among his fellow-warriors by angry envious words and idle tales of detraction; at other times he would burst out openly in his presence and spit his venom upon him. But a wretch who pours out harmful stuff drinks what he gives to drink; and rightly so, when, as in this case, the cup wickedly proffered by the poisoner, charming ever so unwisely,[13] could gratify the taste of nobody, but, as it should have displeased, did rightly displease the lips of all. Finding no welcome, the cup slips back to the cup-bearer, to intoxicate his foiled fury and eager guile against an innocent neighbor. His obstinate and wicked rage is more and more inflamed, his insane fury intensifies itself, until at last it knows not how to put out the fierce fire which it has stirred up. Even so a time came, when this bad knight, driven on by his own heat and excited by his own rancor, made a violent attack upon Aelred in full court in the king's presence. From the outset he donned the helmet of shamelessness; his filthy and unknightly language, which horrified his hearers, was like the outpouring of a railing prostitute. He protested that Aelred was unworthy to have the disposal of the king's treasure and to be in his personal service and enjoy such praise and distinction. He then proceeded to vomit abuse against the elect of the Lord and the heir of future felicity, but I pass his words over in silence—they were too foul for me to speak or for others to hear. Who would believe our report if they were told, or listen if they were written? Or who, indeed, would bear in patience the injury inflicted on so kind, so sweet, so wise, so gentle a friend even of his enemies? But then you might have seen our Aelred, with a blush, deprecate the confusion, not of himself, but of the reviler. He did not hurl recriminations at the blasphemer, but, with words of pure truth, which deserve enduring record, he met with gentle patience this drunkard in iniquity. 'You say well, excellent knight,' he replied, 'you say well and everything you say is true; for, I am sure, you hate lying and love me. Who indeed is worthy to fight for King David, or to serve him as he should be served? I know only too well, and hold myself in deep displeasure, that I am a sinner, and have failed much in my service, not to the king whom I serve on earth, but to the King of Heaven.' O tongue of gold! O mouth, never, may it please God, to be gnawed by worms! Monks should read and reread this passage, and most of all his own monks that they may alike know and understand what this tree, which afterwards brought forth such perfect fruit, was like when it was first planted. O my God, could any tell, as they should be told, the greatness, the efficacy, the worth of this pattern among men? It is not as though he was already living in the cloister; he was in the land of Egypt, where murmuring rather than thanksgiving was wont to be heard, not the voice of the turtle-dove but the noise of the hissing of serpents. Who of those who have learned patience in the seclusion of the cloister during twenty, or even forty, years would reply so patiently, so affectionately, so kindly to one of his companions under the shock of such an assault? This and other like excellencies bound him still closer in the bonds of love to his lord the king and made him to be held by all still dearer in sincere affection, so that the king increasingly confided in him and entrusted him with business of importance. The king saw very clearly that such wholesome outpourings of rare humility and other graces could have no other source than in streams of exceptional prudence and wisdom. The great counsellor had a fitting name, for the English *Alred* is in Latin *totum consilium* or *omne consilium*. Well is he placed in the counsels of an earthly king, whose very name gives forth the sound, 'all counsel', he who was afterwards to be father, counsellor, judge and protector of many servants of God, first showing an example of justice to his companions in the world, then in loftier regions of a more exacting life the pattern even to spiritual men of perfection and inward humility.

The man who had so shamefully reviled him in the presence of the king, and had so often done what he could to disgrace him, began to reflect on the fact that Aelred was not injured or disturbed or hurt in character and esteem, but on the contrary, acquiring greater merit, was lifted to wisdom's peak, growing in well-being every hour as in a happy upward flight, and indeed was, so to

speak, inexpressibly the better for the varied malice with which
he had been so mad as to assail him. Though rather late in the day,
he was led by remorse to seek forgiveness. In a private interview
he promised to be Aelred's firm friend in the future, and that he
would ever abhor, in humility, every presumption of ill-will, and
would most diligently show him peculiar veneration. Our Aelred
replied, 'My brother, I confess that I rejoice with you in your
penitence, I am glad and happy with you in your recovery, and
I am grateful with you for your affectionate feelings; but I love
you and always shall love you much the more because by your
hatred I grew in the love of my lord, and because I have become,
it may be, a little more pleasing to God in the patience which by
this means was stirred and tested in me.' Who will not marvel at
these things? Who will not be astounded? Who will not rejoice to
hear? Behold a new Joseph in Egypt, a second Daniel in Babylon,
a later Lot in Sodom. What can I add? Here indeed is something
to gladden the ears of the peacemakers, which they will fulfil in
their works and so be made blessed. And so, after all the slights
and insults and reviling in public and private, at last, after this
indescribable bewilderment of deep-seated folly, the Solomon of
our time[14] began to be so fond of him who did these things that
he gave him the first place among his friends, and, as though it
had been said to him 'Friend, go up higher',[15] he was every day
loaded with kindness by the humble Aelred as a colleague, praised
as his dearest and made to rejoice as his neighbor.[16]

CHAPTER 4. AELRED'S DESIRE FOR THE CLOISTER

But now God willed that for the welfare and comfort of
many he should give himself more strictly to the way of quiet
and holiness and, so to speak, enter into his chamber where the
floods of the evil world do not flow and the tempest of the sea is
not roused, where there is no rushing of storms and whirlwinds
and the burning winds do not scatter the branches of the vines,
where dust is not stirred to afflict the eyes nor does the deep mire
drag back the steps of those who walk, but where the voice of the
turtle dove is heard, the voice of rejoicing and salvation,[17] where

a new song is sung, the song of Sion, and a continual Alleluia,
where the heart of man is rejoiced by the wine of gladness and is
drunken with the sweet wine of a pure conscience; God willing,
I say, by his grace to call his servant to this laudable and happy
state, inspired him to despise the vainglory of this wicked life
and to make profession of the religious life of an accepted kind,
and, making nought of all earthly counsel, ties and duty, to put the
King of Glory before a prince of flesh and blood. In his cogitation
on these things and how he could the more speedily, fully and
profitably put them in practice, he realized that the monastic life
was the perfect way to receive the heavenly promises; but, fearing
to give open expression to his joyful intention, lest he should be
disturbed by his fear for his lord and suffer delays, he concealed his
determination before the prince and stilled the healthy operation
of his sworn intention with the medicine of dissimulation.[18] In the
meantime the heat of his desire invades his heart, fills his mind,
takes possession of his soul, stays all his senses in the effort not
to seem the man that he is, and wishes to be and to become.
His bones stiffen as his marrow melts away, his flesh withers, the
pulse beats slow, his whole body trembles and his spirit grows
faint in the wretchedness of suspense. The hero of the Lord in his
plight continually prays his Creator that with the goodwill of his
lord he may escape from the slippery passage of the world and be
counted worthy to join the monastic society. And the Lord who
delivers him that is bound from prison, and the blind man from
his darkness, and raises the poor man from his filth and snatches
the needy from the hand of the mighty comes to the rescue of
His servant. It happened in this way.

CHAPTER 5. AELRED HEARS OF RIEVAULX

Shortly afterwards he was in the neighborhood of the city of
York where he was come on business to the archbishop of the
diocese.[19] By a happy chance he heard tell from a close friend of
his,[20] how, two years or more before, certain monks had come
to England from across the sea, wonderful men, famous adepts
in the religious life, white monks by name and white also in

vesture. For their name arose from the fact that, as the angels might be, they were clothed in undyed wool spun and woven from the pure fleece of the sheep. So named and garbed and gathered together like flocks of sea-gulls,[21] 'they shine as they walk with the whiteness of snow. They venerate poverty, not the penury of the idle and negligent,[22] but a poverty directed by a necessity of the will and sustained by the thoroughness of faith, and approved by divine love. They are welded together by such firm bands of charity that their society is as 'terrible as an army with banners'.[23] Trampling the flowers of the world with the foot of forgetfulness, counting riches and honors as dung, beating with the fist of conscience on the faces of mutable things, spurning fleshly desires and vain glory in food, drink, act, attachment, alike in the abundance and scarcity of goods, running an even course in the fit use of them between right and left they observe at all times a discreet uniformity, using only so much and such means of sustaining life as will just maintain the needs of the body and their fervor in the worship of God. For them everything is fixed by weight, measure and number.[24] A pound of bread, a pint[25] of drink, two dishes of cabbage and beans. If they sup, the remnants of their former meal are dished up again except that, instead of the two cooked dishes, fresh vegetables, if they are to be had, are served. When they rest on their beds, each of them lies alone and girdled, in habit and tunic in winter and summer. They have no personal property; they do not even talk together; no-one takes a step towards anything of its own will. Everything they do is at the motion of the prelate's nod and they are turned aside by a like direction. At table, in procession, at communion and in other liturgical observances, all of them, small and great, young and old, wise and ignorant are subject to one law. Personal standing is merged in the equality of each and all, there is no inequitable mark of exception, except the greater sanctity which is able to put one man above others. The only test of worth is the recognition of the best. The humbler a man is the greater he is among them, the more lowly in his own esteem the more pleasing, in the opinion and judgement of the rest.[26] Women, hawks and dogs, except those ready barkers used to drive away thieves from houses, do not enter the gates of their monastery. By their exceeding love they stifle among them the bane of impatience, and every growth of anger and the smoky emanations of pride, and so, in the words of the *Acts of the Apostles,* by the grace and love of the Holy Spirit they are made 'of one heart and of one soul'.[27]

Well, as I have said, these holy men reached England safely from their monastic wrestling ground across the sea. They set up their huts near Helmsley, the central manor of their protector, Walter Espec, a very notable man and one of the leading barons of King Henry I. The spot was by a powerful stream called the Rie in a broad valley stretching on either side. The name of their little settlement and of the place where it lies was derived from the name of the stream and the valley, Rievaulx.[28] High hills surround the valley, encircling it like a crown. These are clothed by trees of various sorts and maintain in pleasant retreats the privacy of the vale, providing for the monks a kind of second paradise of wooded delight. From the loftiest rocks the waters wind and tumble down to the valley below, and as they make their hasty way through the lesser passages and narrower beds and spread themselves in wider rills, they give out a gentle murmur of soft sound and join together in the sweet notes of a delicious melody. And when the branches of lovely trees rustle and sing together and the leaves flutter gently to the earth, the happy listener is filled increasingly with a glad jubilee of harmonious sound, as so many various things conspire together in such a sweet consent in music whose every diverse note is equal to the rest. 'His ears drink in the feast prepared for them, and are satisfied.'[29]

Such was the story—and a true story—which Aelred was told by his friend. At this point he exclaimed, 'And where, oh where, is the way to those angelic men, to these heavenly places?' 'Don't be disturbed,' said his friend, 'they are close to you, and you know it not. You have only to ask and they can easily be found.' He replied, '0, how greatly do I desire, how ardently I thirst for the sight of them, and to see for myself what you have told me about that happy place.' 'Go thither,' returned the other, 'but seek first the leave of the archbishop and receive his blessing, and, if you wish, God will satisfy your desire before the sun sets.' Carried

away by eager desire for the things to come he hurries to the
prelate, obtains his leave and blessing, rushes back to his lodging,
mounts his horse, does not stop to go in, and, with the hastiest of
farewells to his hosts, speeds his mount he knows not where. But
his informant makes him follow behind and, spurring their horses
to a gallop, they reach before nightfall the castle of Helmsley, two
miles from Rievaulx. There the lord, Walter Espec, the founder
of the abbey, gave them a triumphant welcome. They spent the
night with him very happily, and as he told him still more about
the life of the monks Aelred's spirit burned more and more with
inexpressible joy.

CHAPTER 7. AELRED ENTERS RIEVAULX

Next morning the lord Walter, accompanied by a few people
of the vicinity, goes with him to the monks. Aelred meets the
prior, the guestmaster, and the keeper of the gate. They take
the young man to prayers, his face washed with tears, his heart
consumed in humble confession to his Lord. After prayers they
preach the word of God. The power of their talk of spiritual
things is almost too great for him to bear. He gives full vent to
the outpourings of his breast; the fountain of his tears gushes forth
like a deluge flooding the earth. His heart of flesh[30] was so full of
pious affections and moist with the dew of continual mercies, that
it was easier to refuse a smile at urbane jests and honest pleasantries
than to restrain his tears at words of admonishment and the talk
that edifies. Yet it was not on that day that the call of the place
made him choose it as his home. He returned with the lord Walter
Espec to the castle and spent another night there, like the last. After
some talk among the company about a number of things they went
to bed until the morning star appeared. Then, aroused from sleep,
he called to his servants to bridle, saddle and harness the horses
and, when all was ready, he said farewell to the most noble Walter
and set out on the journey to his lord, the King in Scotland. Now
he had to pass along the edge of the hill overlooking the valley,
where a road led down to the gate of the monastery, and when
he reached the spot, still aflame with the heat of the Holy Spirit,

that is to say, with the love of the Lord Jesus, he asked one of his servants, whom he called his friend, if he would like to go down to the abbey and learn something more than he had seen the day before. Oh, the mercy of our God, ever to be proclaimed by those who wish to make their home in Christ! Oh, how faithful is our God in clemency and kindness! For, as our father would tell us, if the friend he had asked if he wished to go down to the monastery or not had said 'I have no mind to go', he himself in that hour would not have gone down with him as he actually did. Take note here of the outshining humility of this gentlest of men, whose own will depended on the will of his servant. God indeed opened the mouth of that servant. He said, 'I am for going down,' and what the servant preferred to do the lord decided should be done. So they went down to the monastery of Rievaulx. Today as yesterday the prior, with the guestmaster, and the keeper of the gate and a great company of the brethren hasten to meet him and do him honor. They have a shrewd suspicion that the will of the visitor, who has come to them again, has been prompted by longing for his well-being; and, since he listens to their words with an eager and unreserved attention, making them his own with tears as things to be embraced, they are led on to probe his mind with more searching admonitions. I need say no more. He agrees at last to become a monk. They all rejoice and are glad together. There was no more dissembling for him, now that his duty has been made clear. He divided all his goods, he abandoned everything that be had. He kept beside him only the one man of his company who was not unwilling to stay. As he owned to me afterwards, the four days of waiting where he was were like a thousand years, so great was his longing and haste to be taken to the novices' cell. He had no eyes for the light of day; all that time he saw only the horror of night. All the same, during those four days, though he could find small pleasure in the companionship of the monks, he greatly edified the brethren in the guesthouse by the humility with which he prostrated himself at the feet of all, the fervent charity with which he burned to serve them, the wisdom with which he talked to them so effectually of the divine commands.[31]

CHAPTER 8. AELRED IN THE NOVITIATE

When the four days were ended he was borne off to the novice-house;[32] but first he was brought before the whole convent to be examined about his intention, and there, as elsewhere, he moved all to tears by the grace of the replies which proceeded out of his mouth. It is not easy for me to speak of him as he was in the novice-house; for there earth was turned to gold. His teacher in that school still lives, Simon, abbot of Sartis, a notable monk.[33] Weary with age, he draws nearer and nearer to the prize;[34] yet in the meanwhile let him speak of our dearly beloved father Aelred in the house of the novices. Speak, old man, speak, speak the truth about him, while you are alive to do so. Do not fear the saying, 'Praise no man while he is alive,[35] for he is already asleep in the Lord and has gone to heaven.' 'In truth', he says, 'he was my companion, not my pupil, and by his assiduity he excelled his teacher in that school'. So you, good old man, you, who made him better than yourself, proclaim him as your superior in the good life. Tell us when and where. When? In the days of his young manhood when the heat of the blood so often erases the mind and clouds the feelings and burns away the energy. Where? In the testing place of his novitiate, where a man finds it so hard to stamp out the old and endure the present and make precaution against future vices. But let the old man speak further of what he knew. Let him say, or rather I will say what I have heard him tell, not once or twice, but seven times and more.

'He was a good man and a man of virtue when still a novice, at the stage when what is old and deep-rooted or new and unexpected are all too often in many an obstacle to virtue. These things in no way held him back even as a novice from virtue. During the time of his training in Christ he excelled all his comrades and fellow-soldiers in humility and glowed in piety. Indeed, it was as you may see a single lamb in a flock of sheep, not any lamb but a little he-lamb, submitting himself to every sheep and in every movement and wriggle of his whole body, paying flattering attentions to all of them. Just so have I watched him attentively wait upon all the novices with whom he lived, abase himself utterly in their ranks, and above human measure in his humanity to the rest. The most remarkable thing in one who exceeded all in the other virtues was a charity which won the victory over himself. Every time he submitted the preference of his own will to the need of another he won this victory. If I were to tell all the occasions when he did this, a sort of miracle, indeed, a sort of martyrdom— for it is a martyrdom and a very great and outstanding one to silence one's soul for a brother's sake, as it is written, "Greater love has no man than this, that a man lay down his life *(animam)* for his friends,"[36] for this is indeed to lay down one's soul for a neighbor—if, I say, I were to set out all the occasions on which he fulfilled this, lack of time would impose silence upon me before I had reckoned them.'

But, as I am in much haste, I pass much by, and deliberately consign to oblivion some of the infinite detail, lest by piling up the riches in too long a work I should weary the reader. So let us make Aelred a monk forthwith.

CHAPTER 9. AELRED MAKES PROFESSION

When a whole year had passed by in the cell where the tyros of Christ are proven, he confirmed his dedication of himself by his written profession before the altar in the church[37] in the presence of all, as the blessed Benedict commands.[38] There he is vested in the sacred robe, that is the cowl sanctified by the abbot's blessing, and henceforth is regarded as a member of the community. And, as he was, like David, somewhat 'ruddy, and with all of a beautiful countenance and goodly to look to,'[39] he gave great delight to the eyes of those who looked upon him. Those early days of his warfare he adorned with the three marks of the monastic life: holy contemplation, sincere prayer and honest toil. Never was he to be found unengaged in one or other of these three things, and he delighted in them 'as in all riches'.[40] Either he was meditating on the divine law or beseeching his God or doing some profitable task. First let us see him in the first duty and show forth the objects of his meditation.

CHAPTER 10. AELRED IN MEDITATION

He did not let his thoughts wander among earthly forms, on the bigness of the unmoved or the number of the movable, or among castles and townships and the other things which pass away. His heart was fixed on him who made all things. The force of his mind was directed where there are no passing thing to flow by, no vain things to end in smoke, where the things that perish make no clamor and hurtful things do not take their stand. The whole strength of his mind was poured out like a flood upon God and his Son; it was as though he had fastened to the crucified Christ a very long thread whose end he had taken back as far as the seat of God the Father. By this thread I mean the strain and concentrated vigor of his mental being. He always remembered and strove after that which made us when we were not and, when we were evil, made us over again to be good. Whenever he considered the beauty, order or worth of the created, he saw in the transitory him who is not able to pass away, 'with whom is no variableness neither shadow of turning'.[41] In his reflections about the world of material creation and its agreement in variety he realized how wonderful was the Creator of beings which, weak and beyond counting, yet possess to the utmost, throughout and in their totality, the grace of harmonious beauty and the power to bear good fruit and an innate capacity to propagate their successors.

Contemplation brought him to the certain assurance that, when all is said, no thing that is made, even though it endures for only the briefest moment of time, but is made by the foresight and wish of God, who so guides and directs every creature to its own peculiar being that all things are as they are seen to be. Moreover, as he pursued this line of thought he saw clearly that every creature in this world has been created for the sake of man alone, and how, if man had been steadfast in the good, they in their turn would not have suffered corruption; for, by his change for the worse, they also fell. When man sinned every creature fell also to a feeble and transitory condition of being. And so, in the course of his meditation, Aelred came to the reformation of the whole world by the grace of Christ, when 'he shall deliver up the Kingdom to God, even the Father', and God shall be 'all in all'.[42] He would end his reflections under what I may describe as the twofold direction of fear and love, the one to the lowest regions, the other to the heavenly mansions, saying in his heart: He is to be feared who has the power to cast into hell-fire,[43] and he is to be loved who is able to raise him who has perished and to crown him in heaven. These were the themes of our father's contemplation, and he meditated on them and in them day and night and turned his heart to them.

CHAPTER 11. AELRED AT PRAYER

His prayer was salted with wisdom. He savored nothing that was bitter and tasted nothing that was savorless, but drinking with joy old wine and new, refused all that was bad. For, so he would say, in prayer there should be no thought of flies, winged beasts, beasts of the earth, people. Let God, he said, be there in the midst, and no other. Only two meet together in prayer, the person and God himself. If a third is present, the cause is not heard as is fitting nor granted as it ought to be, for, as you seek one thing only when you beset God in prayer, so, if you should seek anything from God which you should not, or think in your prayer of something other than that which you seek, you will not have one with you but two against you. He scarce ever prayed without tears; tears, he would say, are the signs of perfect prayers, the embassies between God and man. They show the whole feeling of the heart and declare the will of God to the soul. Prayer without tears is not strong enough to pierce the clouds of heaven, without tears its petitions lose heat, dry up and wither, without tears prayer beats on indifferent ears, so that they do not heed the words of the parched soul. When our Aelred talked with his God he bathed his whole face with a fountain of tears. Then was he sure to placate the countenance[44] of Majesty if he appeared in his sight bathed in these waters. Hence he extinguished with tears all the heat of carnal attachments, and, when he desired to pray, made himself light and easy for the leap to heaven. And so it was that as he wrestled in prayer, despising the earth and everything on the earth, himself most of all, he would often go up into the mountain to greet God, suspended, as it were, between heaven and earth and saying, 'Lord, remember that I am dust, but the wind of your love, the breath of your Holy Spirit has borne me so far; turn me not back nor hurl me down, for it is good and pleasant to be here.' And God, seeing and hearing him thus, would answer, 'My son, he flies easily who flies to God; be it unto you as you have asked'. So comforted was he by this assurance, so drunk with the wine of unspeakable joy, that he could scarce bring himself to come down; indeed after such prayer and such wholesome rapture he would be tired and sad, as though he had come from great toil, and lament the hurt of the descent and sigh as he reflected on the glory of the assumption. But 'steady, steady'.[45] He rises quickly nor sits long in the same place, but hastens to some labor of his hands.

CHAPTER 12. AELRED AT MANUAL WORK

See how he set about this, to the grace of the brethren and his own well-being. Not with noisy show before the others, with unseemly fuss, jostling the monks on all sides and banging the shoulders of the brethren, but turning gaily to what he was told to do, with a glad mind and praiseworthy activity, humble in heart, orderly in the play of his body. He begins and ends the task just as he is bidden, neither more nor less. Always, so far as was in his power, he labored in everything so to perform his superior's command that he should neither exceed it by doing too much nor come short by doing too little. He approached every action without delay, pride or reluctance; he never slackened in his obedience by asking the prior to excuse him a task or to let him do something else, but strove in the constancy of charity to fulfil every order, and with an eagerness of spirit greater than his bodily strength he longed to do more than he could. And with it all he displayed such deftness that even the slack and negligent, when they saw him, were stirred to endure the sweat of honest toil. Weak though he was in body, his splendid spirit carried him through the labors of stronger and strenuous men. He did not spare the soft skin of his hands, but manfully wielded with his slender fingers the rough tools of his field-tasks to the admiration of all.[46] His masters were frequently moved by compassion at the sight to tighten the reins of this most valiant beast of burden of our Saviour Christ.

CHAPTER 13. A SUMMARY OF AELRED'S QUALITIES AS A MONK

So the soldier of Christ, unsubdued, found life and nourishment in these exercises and virtues. Like a busy bee flitting about the meadows of virtue he filled the storeroom of his heart with three sorts of things: honey, oil, and butter;[47] the honey of the contemplation by which he drank in the pleasures of heaven, the oil of piety which made him shine, the butter of compassion for his neighbor, for whose sins he poured out his prayers to God. In contemplation he tasted the honey in which is tasted and seen the sweetness of the Lord, as it is said, 'Taste and see that the Lord is good'.[48] Through piety he found the light of the mercy of the Lord, for piety glows in mercy as oil makes the surface shine. In compassionating his neighbor he ate butter, for, just as butter melts when it is placed near the fire, so compassion loosed in the help of a neighbor refreshes the feeble soul. The prophet means this when he says, 'Spare me that I may recover strength before I go hence and am no more.'[49]

CHAPTER 14.
A MISSION TO ROME. AELRED BECOMES NOVICE MASTER (1142–43)

While Aelred so prospered in the monastic life his abbot, the lord William,[50] observing his labor and solicitude for the good, determined to admit him to the intimacies of his counsel and to the discussion of matters closely affecting the household of Rievaulx. He discovered that Aelred was ten times as wise and prudent as he had supposed, and that he revealed an unexpected ease in the solution of hard, difficult and important problems. The venerable William had no fears about the good issue if Aelred had had early cognisance of a case; for, made aware of the facts, he was like a second Daniel in disentangling cases and coming to a prudent decision. When the abbot sent him to Rome on the famous case of the dissension at York[51] he was received so graciously by the Lord Pope, and expounded the business and brought it to conclusion with such energy, that the esteem and admiration which he won after his return was widespread.

It was then that the lord William put him in charge of the novices, to make them worthy vessels of God and acceptable to the Order and even examples of perfection to those who truly yearn to excel as patterns of goodness. This he did and made good monks of them; some are still alive to testify, as much by the sweetness of their character as by the living voice to his praiseworthy industry. Their manner of life is such that they seem to bear blossoms more dazzling white than the white flowers about them and reveal a yet greater loveliness of incomparable grace. To show by one instance the compassion in his heart and his perfection in the religious life, let those hear who wish to hear what he did, or rather what God, working through him, did, for a certain brother.

CHAPTER 15. A SECULAR CLERK FINDS MOANSTIC LIFE TOO HARD.

In that time there came to Rievaulx a secular clerk who wished to acquire the name and standing of a monk. He was received first in the guest-house, and shortly afterwards in the cell of the novices when Aelred was teaching as master. This clerk was a man with no mental stability, always staggering about, now here, now, there, from one thing to another, shaken like a reed by the wind of his changeful will. Aelred, merciful man, was distressed by this and, in his pity for the fellow, said to God in his heart, '0 Lord, my God, give this man's soul to me and be graciously pleased to grant to me, unworthy though I am, the small hope of salvation that he has.' O outcome of virtue! O most merciful omnipotence of divine clemency! Not long after that brother, a problem in the house of probation and enslaved in his own reprobation, conceived a desire to descend into Egypt[52] and to quit the good purpose which he had begun. So he came and told his master about the unlawful thing, showed the commotion in his mind and unrolled the desire of his evil thoughts. Aelred pleaded with him, 'Brother, do not will your destruction; for you cannot, even although you wish; and it is folly to will the opposite of what all the saints desire.' But, not heeding the counsel of salvation, he left the monastery, unknowingly ignorant, shallowly unconstructed.[53] All day long, after he had passed through the outer enclosures of the monastery, he wandered aimlessly about the woods until, shortly before sunset, he came to the road by which he had left and suddenly found himself again within the monastic wall. His prophet, he who had begged God for his soul, catching sight of him, ran to meet him, put his arms round his neck, kissed his face, and exclaimed, 'Son, why have you thus dealt with me?[54] I have wept many tears for you today. And, as I believe in God, I believe that, as I have sought from the Lord and have promised you, you shall not perish.'

Oh, how shall we magnify you, man of mercy! For all through that day he did not tell even the abbot about this aberration on the part of the brother, fearing lest the holy father's severity to him when he came back might do him hurt, and hoping with prophetic insight that his return would do him good. And it so happened; for, through Aelred's sincerity in prayer, that brother ended his life clothed in his sacred habit, in Aelred's hands.[55]

CHAPTER 16. THE SPRING IN THE NOVITIATE

I should not omit to tell how he had built a small chamber of brick under the floor of the novice-house, like a little tank, into which water flowed from hidden rills. Its opening was shut by a very broad stone in such a way that nobody would notice it. Aelred would enter this contrivance, when he was alone and undisturbed, and immerse his whole body in the icy cold water, and so quench the heat in himself of every vice.

CHAPTER 17. *THE MIRROR OF CHARITY*

During this same time he began to write to various personages letters most lucid in sense and distinguished in style. He also wrote what in my judgement is the best of all his works, the *Mirror of Charity*, as he called it, in three books, which contains as good a picture of the love of God and one's neighbor as a man can see of himself in a mirror.[56] And at this point I wish, with God's help, to describe briefly and clearly the quality of his fine and acute mind.

CHAPTER 18. AELRED'S INTELLECTUAL QUALITIES.

He had indeed been given, as he retained, natural capacity to a high degree. Of course he retained it, he who, having acquired but little knowledge in the world,[57] knew so much afterwards, and knew so well what he did know. He felt rather than absorbed what the authorities call the liberal arts, by the process of oral instruction in which the master's voice enters the pupil's breast; but in all other respects he was his own master, with an understanding far beyond that of those who have learned the elements of secular knowledge from the injection of words rather than from the infusion of the Holy Spirit. These acquire from their teacher a hazy idea of Aristotelian forms and the infinite reckonings of Pythagorean computation; but he, by the rapidity of his genius flying through the world of numbers and transcending every figure of speech, both real and feigned, knew in the Scriptures, and taught, him who alone has immortality, where there is no number, and dwells in light inaccessible where there is no figure but the very truth which, rightly understood, is the goal of all earthly knowledge. He never sought to involve his speech in the deceitful trappings which burden rather than enhance the value of its sense, because they rob truth of its meaning by digressions which it does not require and by additions which it disdains. For truth is self-contained; it needs no verbal artifice to explain and drive it home. Just as the sun, in order to shine, has no need for anything to make it shine more than it does shine, but would shine the less by any alien addition to it, so, to anyone who knows how to see it, the truth is sufficient in itself alone: if you impose something else upon it or mix something else with it, it becomes the less convincing just in so far as folly presumes to buttress up its inherent worth by what is foreign to it. Words acquire their full force only from reason, which is itself the element in truth, so to speak, and which gives to anything good its persuasive, appealing or convincing quality. Verbiage can be meaningless, in no way different from the barking of a dog. This is why I say that our father refused to put the rules of grammar before the truth, but everywhere put truth before them. He despised the vain pursuit of eloquence and preferred the pure, undiluted truth of the matter about which he might be speaking. At the same time he did not convey any impression of uncouthness in expression, but had at his command all the resources of splendid eloquence and a noble flow of words. He was ready and easy in speech, said what he wished to say and said it well. But enough of this. His writings, preserved for posterity by the labor of my own hand, show quite well enough how he was wont to express himself. Let us now proceed to what follows.

CHAPTER 19. THE FOUNDATION OF REVESBY

The house of Rievaulx conceived a third daughter[58] in her womb and showed signs that the time of her labor was drawing near. And when she gave birth, the midwives chose Aelred as bearer and nurse of the latest lusty addition to the family, declaring that, nourished by the milk of his solicitude, it would quickly grow into a stout child. And so it was. How? The brethren sent from Rievaulx to a place in Lindsey, twenty miles from the royal city of Lincoln, elected him as their abbot.

CHAPTER 20. REVESBY UNDER AELRED'S RULE (1143–47)

After his arrival with them in this place he rapidly and powerfully increased by the grace of Jesus Christ the number of the brethren. The abbey has two names—one, Saint Lawrence, from the name of the saint to which the church of the place where the abbey was built was formerly dedicated (the church is still there); the other Revesby, the name of the township. In this place the holy father made miraculous progress. As he sweats in exhausting and endless labors on behalf of his tender little flock, he is comforted by God and made glad by his manifold blessing. His fame runs

through the whole countryside. Bishop, earls, barons venerate the
man and the place itself, and in their reverence and affection load
it with possessions, heap gifts upon it and defend it by their peace
and protection. The bishop orders him to preach to the clergy in
their local synods and he does so; to bring priests to a better way of
life, as he does not fail to do; to accept grants of land from knights
in generous free-alms, and he obeys, since he had realized that in
this unsettled time such gifts profited knights and monks alike, for
in those days it was hard for any to lead the good life unless they
were monks or members of some religious order, so disturbed and
chaotic was the land, reduced almost to a desert by the malice,
slaughters and harryings of evil men.[59] And so he desired that that
land, for which almost all men were fighting to the death, should
pass into the hands of the monks for their good; and he knew
that to give what they had helped the possessors of goods to their
salvation, and that, if they did not give, they might well lose both
life and goods without any payment in return. And so the servant
of the Lord, greatly beloved by all in the province, indeed by the
whole realm and most of all by the king, made his house rich and
fruitful. Within, the religious life waxed every hour and grew day
by day; without, possessions increased and gave a regular return in
money and means for all kinds of equipment. For God was in that
house and the Lord blessed it greatly. There was no sterility there,[60]
for our Jacob beget twins by both Leah and Rachel, as he preached
fear and justice to the administrative staff and impressed the duties
of prayer and love upon the contemplatives in the cloister, saying
to the former, 'Fear the Lord, ye his saints, for there is no want
in them that fear him,' and to the latter, 'They who dwell in
your house, O Lord, shall be always praising you.'[61] And here I
must write something about the miracles which God worked there
through his servant Aelred.

CHAPTER 21. AELRED CURES THE SUB-PRIOR OF REVESBY

The sub-prior of the house, a God-fearing and religious man,
had long been the victim of very sharp attacks of fever. His vital
force was so sapped by their immoderate heat, his veins were so

dried up, that he could scarce retain the panting breath in his body. His frame was so wretchedly wasted that it looked like the hollowed woodwork of a lute; eyes, face, hands, arms, feet, shins, blotched and misshapen, proclaimed that the death agony was drawing nearer and nearer. Only his voice begging God for a longer lease of life prevailed over matter in the man. So the sick man lay upon his bed, his limbs scarcely holding together, for the contraction and loosening of his joints and nerves made them leap from the sockets of his bones, and only the thin layer of fragile skin kept his body together, though hardly able, as his weakness grows upon him, to prevent it from falling entirely to pieces. But notice! the holy father comes into the infirmary and visits the sick-beds one by one, and at last comes to him and, looking upon him, utterly refuses to allow such a loss to the house, and such a distressing state of body; and so at length he says to him as he lies there, 'Tomorrow, in the name of the Lord, make your way to the church, take your place in the choir of psalmodists, sing with them, and pray to God; and through him, I believe, you will be well.' When morning came the brother did as he had bidden, and to his joy everything happened as Aelred had promised. The old gave place to a happier new; unlooked-for health triumphed over the long wastage of the fever. He suddenly became a strong cheerful man. He lived henceforth as he had been wont to live long ago, clinging in ever-growing affection to the holiness, proved for his sake, of the father.

CHAPTER 22. THE UNSTABLE MONK AGAIN

In this same time the same brother to whom I have referred above, he whose soul Aelred had begged God to give him, was again caught in the fire of his former instability, and wished to leave the monastery. Coming to the Abbot he made his application in these terms: 'Lord, my inconstancy is not equal to the burden of the Order. Everything here and in my nature are opposed to each other. I cannot endure the daily tasks. The sight of it all revolts me. I am tormented and crushed down by the length of the vigils, I often succumb to the manual labor. The food cleaves to my mouth, more bitter than wormwood. The rough clothing cuts through my skin and flesh down to my very bones. More than this, my will is always hankering after other things, it longs for the delights of the world and sighs unceasingly for its loves and attachments and pleasures.' Hearing this the noble director replied, 'And I am prepared to give you better food to eat and softer raiment and to grant you every indulgence allowable to a monk, if only you will persevere and bring yourself to live with me in the monastery.' 'I would not stay,' he replied, 'though you gave me all the wealth of this house.' To whom Aelred, 'And I, in my turn, taste no food till the Lord brings you back, willing or unwilling.' The one runs to the gate to depart, the other enters his chamber to pray. The most pious father pours out lamentations for his son, and mourns for the wanderer with deep and heartfelt sighs and refuses to be comforted. For the sub-cellarer, his nearest kinsman, comes to him and says, 'Why on earth do you cry out your eyes for that wretched creature? And is it true that you have vowed to starve yourself to death if he does not come back?' The saint, 'What is that to you? Do not, I beseech you, add sorrow to my sorrow, for I am tormented in this flame[62] and, unless help comes to my son, I die. What is that to you?' Meanwhile the fugitive comes to the gate, hastening to get away, but at the open doors he felt the empty air as though it were a wall of iron. Again and again he tries with all his might to break through and get out, but every effort was in vain and willy-nilly he gets no farther. At last, in intense rage he takes hold of the hinges of the gate with both hands and, stretching out his leg, tries to put one foot forward, but in no way did he contrive to reach even the boundary. Then all who were there execrate the fellow's ingratitude to God and magnify the love of the father Aelred who, though the gates were open, had shut the air against him and would not allow him to fall into the pit of iniquity. But he, contrite and brought back to himself, quickly returns to the most pious protector, seeks his pardon, promises to be firm. To whom the saint, 'Bravo, my son, you have well come. Truly my God, who has brought you back safe, has had compassion on me.' Let all true lovers of Aelred read this miracle over and over again.

CHAPTER 23. THE BROTHER CURED BY AELRED'S STAFF

In this same time there was a certain brother, a skilled crafts-man of the monastery, who had injured an arm so grievously that his whole body seemed likely to be affected in the same deadly way. For the shock of the injury, affecting the whole limb, had given it a threefold twist back on itself like a ram's horn, and paralyzed and contorted the hand beneath, so that he could never rest in bed on that side of his body because of the suffering with which the injured limb affected all others. He was a simple, religious soul, a man of great faith, and when one day he entered the church for Mass and noticed the abbot's staff set in a wooden stand by the door, he ventured to find a cure in the staff by the merits of the blessed man and the grace of Jesus Christ. For, taking it in his sound hand he passed it three times in a circle about the sick limb, making the sign of the cross three times. At the third movement and the third life-giving sign his arm immediately shot back to its normal length, his hand resumed its natural mobility and health removed all his discomfort.

CHAPTER 24. THE DEATH OF WILLIAM OF RIEVAULX (1145)

While the venerable father Aelred shone in the magnificent radiation of these and many other miracles and virtues, death, the last enemy, closed the life on earth of the lord William, abbot of Rievaulx.[63] His life is indeed to be blessed, for 'the Lord gave him his blessing and confirmed his covenant on his head.'[64] From him, as from an inexhaustible well, streams of the religious life have watered those who have come after him, and to this day flow and overflow in full measure in the house of Rievaulx and in her daughters, grateful and pleasant to drink, wholesome and of unfailing efficacy to lave those who are weak.

CHAPTER 25. MAURICE, SECOND ABBOT OF RIEVAULX (1145–47)

Maurice succeeded him, a man of great sanctity and of out-standing judgement, befitting one who from boyhood had drunk the wine of spiritual gladness in the cloister at Durham, and, refreshed by the bread of Cuthbert, that man of God, had climbed so high as to be called by his companions a second Bede; and truly in his day, by his pre-eminence both in life and learning he alone could be compared with Bede. I myself have seen this man and knew him well, and I know how few men of his quality the world of mortal men contains. But, irked by the uneasy burdens of the pastoral care, he resigned his stewardship after two years and preferred to resume his seat in the cloister.[65]

CHAPTER 26. AELRED IS ELECTED THIRD ABBOT OF RIEVAULX (1147)

Aelred was duly chosen by the brethren in his place, and now began to shine more brightly than ever. Like the sun at noonday he spread still more widely the clearness of his light. There are some who think that ambition brought him to the headship of this house. Every good man knows that this is false. That his virtue provoked jealous men to lie is not surprising—virtue never fails to stir envy—and how many jealous busybodies this man of peace had to endure! Some few of them are still alive, but his death, so 'precious in the sight of the Lord,'[66] has cut away the error of his detractors. And in his life also he stilled his monsters;[67] for the malignant and misguided men who rose up against him were indeed as monsters; they spoke lies with their tongue against the just and the 'pride of those who hated him rose up continually'.[68] Some said that he was a good man, others, 'No, he is a glutton and a wine-bibber and a friend of publicans,[69] and gives up his body to baths and ointments.' To which I reply:

CHAPTER 27. WALTER DANIEL'S REPLY TO AELRED'S CRITICS

He used to eat what was set before him as a sick man who was greatly afflicted, and so sparingly that those who loved him found it hard to believe that he was a man and not a spirit. He would occasionally drink wine because of his old malady the stone, which grievously tormented him every month, in accordance with the advice of the Apostle to Timothy, 'Use a little wine for thy stomach's sake and thine often infirmities.'[70] The agony was intense, for very often his urine contained fragments of stone as big as a bean, the passage of which was so unbearable that if in his suffering he had not tempered and softened the obstruction in the bath to ease its course he would have incurred sudden death. One day, after no less than forty visits to the bath, he was so incredibly exhausted in the evening that he looked more dead than alive. And you dare to talk about the bathings of Aelred! Do you suppose that he took delight when there was so much frustration? He, himself a friend of the sick, the physician who used to relieve them so manfully in their imperfect state and to cure so many! He was not like those of whom the Lord says, 'You took what you saw to be fat, and drove out what was feeble'[71]; rather he made his own the words of the Apostle, 'I will gladly spend and be spent for your souls.'[72]Nor let anyone find it strange that he himself suffered from many bodily infirmities; the Apostle who was the most of all afflicted says, 'When I am weak, then am I strong.'[73] So Aelred was made very strong in his great weakness.

CHAPTER 28. AELRED'S PROPHETIC VISION OF THE DEATH OF
THE UNSTABLE MONK

In truth it was during this time that he saw clearly in a dream what was about to happen to the brother mentioned above, whose departure through the gate into the outside world he prevented by his prayers. For this same brother was nearing home on his return from a mission on which the venerable Aelred had sent him, along with my father Daniel and certain others of the house, to the abbey of Swineshead[74] to illuminate it with the Cistercian way of life. In the night before the day of his return to the gate of Rievaulx, Abbot Aelred was lying on his bed, whether dozing or sleeping 'I cannot tell; God knoweth';[75] and lo! a man of venerable appearance stood beside him and said, 'Father abbot, that monk of yours will arrive at the monastery gate in the morning at the first hour; see that he enters the cloister, for within a few days he will be seized by a severe illness and he will die in your hands.'

Having uttered this prophecy the seer vanished and the holy man awoke from his dream. Night passed, day came, in due course the first hour of light began, and the abbot was told that he of whom the prophecy was spoken was outside the doors of the abbey and begged the father to be so good as to go out to him. The saint gladly obeyed and went down to him; and, when he saw him he kissed him tenderly and, thinking of the vision, shed many sweet tears over him. He bade him to come in and to rejoice with spiritual joy, for 'Soon, very soon,' he said, 'by the will of God you shall be made perfect in glory.' The man, not catching his meaning, smiles and whispers, 'What, shall I enter again on that death without end which the cloistered always endure? No, by your leave, I go at once for a month to visit my kindred to enjoy with them for just a little while the good things of this present world, and so return to you again.'[76] 'Not so, my son,' says the father, 'but come in now, for I live no longer without you, and you shall not die without me.' So with fair words he enticed the monk to come into the monastery with him. On his entrance the abbot rejoiced beyond belief and began to celebrate in his heart a glad, though hidden, feast. Five or six days later the guest[77] fell sick and was struck down by a very serious illness. His nose bled continually; all the brethren begin to despair for his life; the father ran to and fro comforting his son and waiting assiduously on the invalid. After a few days he was afflicted by the pangs of death, and the abbot in the usual way recited the litany[78] for the departing soul; but, as he spoke, he forgot the vision and did not embrace the dying man, so that he twice brought the litany to a close and was compelled to begin it a third time. Then he remembered what he had seen and, taking [the monk's] head in his hands, exclaimed, 'Saint Benedict, pray for him.' And he, as the abbot touched his head and uttered the name of the saint, immediately breathed his last in Aelred's hands. But let us proceed.

CHAPTER 29. RIEVAULX UNDER AELRED

He turned the house of Rievaulx into a stronghold for the sustaining of the weak, the nourishment of the strong and whole;

it was the home of piety and peace, the abode of perfect love of God and neighbor. Who was there, however despised and rejected, who did not find in it a place of rest? Whoever came there in his weakness and did not find a loving father in Aelred and timely comforters in the brethren? When was anyone, feeble in body and character, ever expelled from that house, unless his iniquity was an offence to the community or had destroyed all hope of his salvation? Hence it was that monks in need of mercy and compassion flocked to Rievaulx from foreign peoples and from the far ends of the earth, that there in very truth they might find peace and 'the holiness without which no man shall see God.'[79] And so those wanderers in the world to whom no house of religion gave entrance came to Rievaulx, the mother of mercy, and found the gates open, and entered by them freely, giving thanks unto their Lord. If one of them in later days had taken it upon himself to reprove in angry commotion some silly behavior, Aelred would say, 'Do not, brother, do not kill the soul for which Christ died, do not drive away our glory from this house. Remember that "we are sojourners as were all our fathers,"[80] and that it is the singular and supreme glory of the house of Rievaulx that above all else it teaches tolerance of the infirm and compassion with others in their necessities. And "this is the testimony of our conscience,"[81] that this house is a holy place because it generates for its God sons who are peacemakers. 'All'—he would continue—'whether weak or strong, should find in Rievaulx a haunt of peace, and there, like the fish in the broad seas, possess the welcome, happy, spacious peace of charity, that it may be said of her, "Whither the tribes go up, the tribes of the Lord, unto the testimony of Israel, to give thanks to the name of the Lord."[82] There are tribes of the strong and tribes of the weak. The house which withholds toleration from the weak is not to be regarded as a house of religion. "Your eyes have seen me, yet being imperfect, and in your book all shall be written." '[83]

CHAPTER 30. THE INCREASE IN NUMBERS

I must not omit to mention the extent to which this holy dwelling, the house of Rievaulx, grew under the hand of the venerable father. He doubled all things in it—monks, *conversi*, laymen, farms, lands and every kind of equipment; indeed he trebled the intensity of the monastic life and its charity. On feast days you might see the church crowded with the brethren like bees in a hive, unable to move forward because of the multitude, clustered together, rather, and compacted into one angelical body. Hence it was that the father left behind him at Rievaulx, when he returned to Christ, one hundred and forty monks and five hundred *conversi* and laymen.[84] His material legacy was great enough, under prudent management, to feed and clothe a still greater number, and to leave something over for their successors. He would make 'as though he would have gone further' when he was receiving those who wished to enter the Order, so that as though unwilling he might be prevailed upon to consent to the petitions of the brethren[85]; with the result that very many were received whom he himself did not know, for often he left it to their judgement and discretion to take whom they wished. Indeed he was very diffident, and indulgent to the feebleness of everyone, and would never disappoint anybody who appealed to him in the cause of charity.

CHAPTER 31. THE PRIVILEGE SHOWED AELRED ON ACCOUNT OF HIS BAD HEALTH

Throughout the last ten years of his life this holy man frequently underwent intense suffering, as the agonies of arthritis were added to his old distresses. So dreadfully afflicted was he that I have seen him suspended in mid-air in a linen sheet, held by a man at each of its four corners, being carried to relieve himself or from one bed to another. A mere touch affected him like a piercing wound, and his cries revealed the measure of his pain. Because of his suffering the General Chapter of abbots at Cîteaux allowed him to eat and sleep in the infirmary, and carefully made other needful concessions to his bodily weakness. He was not to hold his office as a chronic invalid, but rather to transact the business of the Order in the convent entirely as he wished—for example, he might sing Mass both in public and private and visit the granges when he wished, recite the regular hours where he preferred in the establishment, go to choir at times different from those prescribed for other abbots, and in various other ways take his part in providing for the well-being of his church.[86] He felt diffident about this generous provision for his freedom, and found it so hard to bear that he ordered a mausoleum to be built for him close by the common infirmary, and, taking up his quarters there, he entrusted the care of his illness entirely to the ministration of two of the brethren, refusing with disdain all dainties and useless blandishments.

The construction of this cottage was, indeed, a great source of consolation to the brethren, for every day they came to it and sat in it, twenty or thirty at a time, to talk together of the spiritual delights of the Scriptures and of the observance of the Order.[87] There was nobody to say to them, 'Get out, go away, do not touch the abbot's bed'; they walked and lay about his bed and talked with him as a little child prattles with its mother. He would say to them, 'My sons, say what you will; only let no vile word, no detraction of a brother, no blasphemy against God proceed out of your mouth.' He did not treat them with the pedantic imbecility habitual in some silly abbots who, if a monk takes a brother's hand in his own, or says anything that they do not like, demand his cowl, strip and expel him. Not so Aelred, not so.[88] I lived under his rule for seventeen years, and in all that time he, merciful as he was above all those who dwell in the world, did not expel a single monk. Four, it is true, left him without his knowledge, but the Lord led them all back save one follower of Satan.[89] In a corner of the cell of which I have spoken he established an inner closet and ordered that it should be closed off by a wooden partition. Here he kept a cross and relics of certain saints, and dedicated it as a place of prayer. And reflecting how 'He who keeps Israel neither slumbers nor sleeps,'[90] he, as God's vicar, slept but little in his bed, but prayed much in that place. There, when his illness allowed him the slightest relief, on bended knees, with contrite mind and in the spirit of truth, he would beset his Father with his prayers.

CHAPTER 32. AELRED'S WORKS

In that abode of his he wrote many memorable works. Indeed, before this period he published a life of David, king of Scotland, in the form of a lamentation, and added to it a genealogy of the king of England, the younger Henry.[91] Also, before that, he sent to Ivo, a monk of Wardon, out of the library of his heart, a noble exposition of the lesson in the gospel beginning 'When Jesus was twelve years old,' a brilliant treatment of the threefold meaning [of Scripture]: historical, moral, and mystical.[92] But it was in that private closet that he wrote and finished with his own hand the thirty-three homilies on the burden of Babylon, in Isaiah,[93] and, after these, other fine and profitable works. Later, he published in three books the dialogue on spiritual friendship.[94] In the first of these he introduced the aforesaid Ivo as the questioner and joined me with himself in the subsequent discussion. And after these he wrote a book to his sister, the chaste virgin who was a recluse, in which he traced the course of this kind of profession from the ardor of the entrance into the same to its perfection.[95] This done, he published the life of the most holy King Edward, a work whose pages shine with the great glory and splendor of the miracles.[96] Next he expounded in honor of the same saint and to be read with the passage at his solemn vigils the gospel lesson which begins, 'No man, when he has lighted a candle, puts it under a bushel but on a candlestick.'[97] He wrote this at the request of his kinsman Lawrence, the abbot of Westminster, and to please the brethren there serving God.[98] After which he finished two books of his work about the soul, that is, its nature, extent and quality, and other matters relating to the soul,[99] and he almost finished the third book, but his end in this life came before he brought it to a close. He paid the debt of all flesh before he had finished it. Throughout the course of this literary activity *(inter hec)* he was sending letters to the lord Pope, to the king of France, the king of England, the king of Scotland, the archbishops of Canterbury and York and nearly every bishop in England, also to the most distinguished men in the Kingdom of England and especially to the Earl of Leicester, letters written with a noble pen to every grade of the ecclesiastical order, in which he left a living image of himself, for what he there commended in writing he himself practiced in life, and lived much better than he could say. Unless I am wrong, he preached about two hundred most eloquent sermons, worthy of all praise, in our chapters, in synods and to the people.[100]

CHAPTER 33. AELRED'S MIRACLES

Such, then, were the fruits put forth by the venerable father, and just as many miracles, of which I now proceed to give a faithful account, are associated with him. For I deem it unjust to show to the readers of this work the brick, wood, brass and iron in which the father abounded in external things, and to be silent about the silver, gold and precious stones[101] in which his spirit exceeded.

CHAPTER 34. A MONK WITH A STOMACHIC DISEASE

A monk suffered extremely from a stomachic complaint. Medical men testify that this is a very dangerous disease: it arises from the worst and most poisonous humors which gather together and solidify in the body, and it is accompanied by biting pains in the stomach; often, when it gets control in the stomach, it may result in sudden death. Well, as I have said, one of the monks was suffering from this disease. He lost his powers of speech and remained dumb many days. The abbot was not at home. When he returned he came to the sufferer and, putting his forefinger on his mouth, said, 'Speak, my brother, in the name of the Lord.' To our amazement he immediately replied, 'Blessed lord, I gladly speak with you.' And at the same time he ceased to feel any pain, and, through the merits of the saint, was restored to perfect health.

CHAPTER 35. THE SHEPHERD WHO WAS DUMB FOR THREE DAYS

One of our shepherds, who had been dumb for three days, was brought to the abbey. Apart from the incapacity of speech, nothing was wrong with him. Set before the abbot he heard him say, 'Speak, I command you in Christ.' What he touched his lips with I do not know, but I do know that he at once broke out into speech.

CHAPTER 36. THE YOUNG MONK WITH HEART FAILURE

A young monk suffered so much from heart failure that he was in danger of death. Unable to see, hear or speak, his end was rapidly drawing near. He had no voice, no use of his faculties; in his intolerable affliction all his members were paralyzed; the only sign of life was a slow respiration through his nostrils, where he seemed to be drawing his last breath. The father in that hour was sitting in the orchard, transacting certain business with the cellarers—I was there with him—when lo! somebody came and told the abbot of the condition of the brother, and added, 'Hasten, lord, before he dies'. Night had set in, and you could discern the old man stumbling along, seeking no aid of the staff which he always used; but, when he reached the poor fellow he thought that he was gone, since where he sought he found no trace of life, for his pulse had ceased to beat. So the master ran, sad and groaning deeply, to his little oratory and gathered together the relics of saints and the text of John's Gospel which, for many years, he had carried about with him, put on a hair-cloth to cover his nakedness,[102] and bore them to the sick man and bound them on his breast, exclaiming with tears, 'Beloved son, may the Son of God make you whole.' And immediately he was relieved of all his trouble.

CHAPTER 37. THE MYSTERIOUS DEATH OF A VITUPERATIVE
ABBOT OF A DAUGHTER-HOUSE

About this time a certain spiritual spouse of one of the daughters of Rievaulx sought her mother on a visitation.[103] This abbot was much too inclined to contumely and was cunningly ill-natured in 'spreading the net in the sight of the birds.'[104] He burst out upon our father and, violently attacking him with darts of cursing and cruelly pursuing him with the arrows of many blasphemies, moved his spirit to indignation against him and deservedly roused him to anger upon him. His unjust presentation of his case turned the dispute against him, for in his eagerness to press it too far he plunged into evil, and in his rebellion against the light he heaped upon himself thick clay,[105] while he supposed that he was darkening the saint's heart, radiating the light of justice. In his resentment against the man's malice the lover of truth lifted his eyes to heaven and, stretching his hand on high, pronounced these terrible words of judgement in answer to his cruel tongue, 'Lord King of everlasting glory, may this man, I beseech thee, speedily suffer an end to his malice, for you know how false are the things which, in his angry folly, he ascribes to my name.' What then? Well, after the mad fellow had relieved his swollen spirit by ejecting the frothy spittle of mendacity upon him he went home without the blessing of the venerable father Aelred, to the great indignation of all the brethren of Rievaulx. And, as the words of saints do not perish, for not one iota of them, as is well known, is spoken without cause, this same person who shortly before had swelled against a just man, had hardly crossed the threshold of his own house when he took to his bed in a pitiable state and seven days later died in agony.

CHAPTER 38. AELRED COPES WITH DISPUTES IN GALLOWAY

After this experience the father went down to Galloway to visit and comfort a daughter-house of Rievaulx. There he found the petty king of that land incensed against his sons, and the sons raging against their father and each other.[106] It is a wild country where the inhabitants are like beasts, and is altogether barbarous. Truth there has nowhere to lay her head,[107] and 'from the sole of the foot even unto the head there is no wisdom in it.'[108] For neither faith nor true hope nor loyal charity for long lasts in it. There chastity founders as often as lust wills, and the pure is only so far removed from a harlot that the more chaste will change their husbands every month and a man will sell his wife for a heifer. Nevertheless some of the men of those parts are turned into monks of a sort, if they have been formed into a religious house, though under the counsel and guidance of others; scarce any have the assiduity to reach perfection of themselves, for they are by nature dull and brutal and so always inclined to carnal pleasures.

Rievaulx made a foundation in this savagery, which now, by the help of God, who gives the increase to a new plantation, bears much fruit.[109] As I have said, our father on a visit to the place found the princes of the province quarrelling among themselves. The king of Scotland could not subdue, nor the bishop pacify, their mutual hatreds, rancor and tyranny. Sons were against father, father against sons, brother against brother, daily polluting the unhappy little land with bloodshed. Aelred the peacemaker met them all and, with words of peace and goodness, bound together the angry sons by a firm peace in a single bond of affection. He eagerly urged their veteran sire to put on the monastic habit and by his marvelous admonishment bent him to that course, and taught him—who had taken the life of thousands—to become a partaker of the life eternal, to such effect that he ended his days in a monastery of religious brethren. Truly, indeed, might it be said of him that 'where the tree falls, there it shall be.'[110] His sons, holding their father in great veneration, live together to this day in peace and tranquillity.[111] After this digression let us return to the miracles.

CHAPTER 39. THE YOUNG MAN WHO SWALLOWED A FROG

So, as on his return from that land, the Lord Aelred was riding with his companions towards Rievaulx he met a young man with a frightfully swollen belly. He was so distended that he seemed to be carrying a cask. His natural form was disgracefully misshapen. You could see the poor wretch wilting under the burden, now falling to the ground, now trying to rise and sinking back again, unable to stand or sit or lie. His face was drawn, his eyes bloodshot, his pupils dimmed. The hairs of his head were like those of a goat rather than of a man, and his head itself was sunk into his monstrous body without any sign of a neck. In his swollen condition the man appeared like a very fat ox or sheep, except that in its natural state this gives general pleasure, whereas he was a terrifying object to everybody.[112] Oh, how truly wretched is the race of humankind! For what was the occasion of this great calamity that had happened to him? It was only a tiny little frog, which he had unwittingly swallowed while he was drinking some water to quench his thirst, and which had grown in his belly and eaten away his entrails day by day, gathering there the wherewithal to live. The food and drink of the weak creature were the coatings of the stomach. Behold, O man, how a little worm, soon to die, cuts into your vitals and you have no power to pluck it out with your hand! Consider what a poor wretch you are. Such are your sons, O Adam. Here kings are powerless; even if they feel them there, they cannot eject frogs from their bellies.

But Aelred was given power over the frog, so that it may come forth from the belly and lose its power. For that poor wretch whom the frog had all but destroyed, falling at the father's feet, said, 'Lord, if you will, you can cure me.'[113] 'No,' replied the humble one, 'but God can cure you if he wills, for when he wills, everything is possible.' And, dismounting from his horse, he inserted two fingers into his mouth and, invoking God, is said to have ejaculated some such words as these: 'Lord King Almighty, I beseech you, by your Son the Lord Jesus, to look upon this your creature, and do to him as you will and know.' Hardly had he uttered the words when, behold, the frog within climbed up on to the fingers which the father had inserted into the man's mouth. When he withdrew his finger joints, the quadruped issues through the door of the mouth and falls to the ground. Its departure is followed all that day by glutinous humors and pus horrible beyond measure; but on the next day every vestige of swelling and pain disappears, and the youth, completely whole, gives thanks to God with all joy and with all due devotion gives praise to the father Aelred by whose kindly intervention he had earned the grace to be healed.[114] Then, resuming his way, the abbot shortly afterwards safely returned to his sons. These things were done four years before his transmigration to heaven.

CHAPTER 40. THE LAST FOUR YEARS OF AELRED'S LIFE

God willing, I shall briefly describe how in those four years, like a second Noah, he compacted the ark of his life within the breadth of a single cubit, and, keeping the fabric of the pure temple, his body, in good repair, renewed and perfected it, and polished all the stones of the spotless sanctuary, his breast, and made them all square, and with the plummet of exact living built them into a house of perfection. We shall not, indeed, describe all the marvels which he is known to have done, but, so far as our ability allows, make note of some remarkable matters and set out a few of the triumphs of the soldier of Christ. For who, however able, eloquent and painstaking, could believe himself competent to give a clear account in words of the virtues of all the works that he did and to publish them to human ears? If he should presume to do so, the very attempt would be the greatest proof of his incapacity, and he would rightly become an object of derision for trying by tale to number the infinite. Certainly I, so poorly and meagerly informed, in no wise believe that I can do the impossible; I set limits to my grasp of the miracles and works of the father, I bow to their infinity, and tell only those which are common knowledge, whose truth is well established and proved by the long experience of those whose praiseworthy life testifies to the truth of their evidence. If this were not so I should prefer complete silence to doubtful truth. Everything I say I saw myself or give from the account of eye-witnesses. Wherefore, since our story is confirmed by the testimony not of two or three but of many religious, pious readers should hold it so much the more dear, as no vestige of error will mar their apprehension of it.

CHAPTER 41. HIS INCREASED AUSTERITY

Throughout those four years[115] before his death, our father experienced what I may call a second circumcision, not by the removal of superfluities which even did not exist, but by depriving himself of necessities very helpful to him in his weakness. He made his little body free of everything that is pleasant in this present life. He sacrificed himself on the altar of unfailing suffering: hardly any flesh clung to his bones; his lips alone remained, a frame to his teeth. The excessive emaciation of his body and the thinness of his face gave an angelic expression to his countenance. Eating scarcely anything and doing less, by his unbelievable fasting he lost altogether, and no wonder, the desire for food. During this period he rejected the curatives which he had been wont to take, and if by chance he tasted anything of that kind in his mouth he took it out with his fingers and, while his attendants were engaged on other things, threw it on the ground and ground it to powder with his foot so that it should not be seen. Nor, as had been his custom, would he take a little wine, but would have it watered and sip, rather than drink, a mixture which was more like water than wine, although the physicians had prescribed pure wine as the particular remedy of his infirmity, asserting that otherwise the disease would take its course and that he would soon die. But the father, taking his soul in his hands, gave greater weight to his own counsels than to those of the physicians, and for God's sake despised the cure of the body and considered in all ways the health of the soul.

CHAPTER 42. HIS PRIVATE DEVOTIONS

From now onwards he armed himself[116] in such unwearied assiduity with prayers and vigils, and plunged so deep into the abyss of contemplation, that very often, shut away in his little oratory, he forgot all about the regular hours and about meals. Even more diligent than had been his custom in reading, prayer and contemplation, he for the most part neglected things present and lived continuously in the things to come. His reading was in edifying books whose words are wont to bring tears, and in particular he generally had in his hands the *Confessions* of Augustine, for it was these which had been his guide when he was converted from the world. He would sit in a kind of grave in the floor of the little oratory and, remembering how he was but dust,[117] he would weep in it every day and say in prayer to God, 'How long, Lord, shall this wretchedness encompass me? How long shall the night, how long the darkness, surround me, how long shall my own vesture abhor me?'[118]

CHAPTER 43. HIS HEAVENLY VISITORS

But our father was not in darkness in that place. Often, throughout those four years, so some declare for a fact, the light of angelic visitation shone there upon his head and he talked with heavenly spirits just as he was wont to talk with men; and when he was alone there many voices used to be heard there, and that place became very dreadful. These visitations of divine grace and angelic conversations made a new man of him, and, as Moses was as though horned when he talked with the divine word,[119] so after his own fashion he revealed by the color of his countenance and a change in his face that he had been in the presence of spiritual agencies of the divine light and had contemplated heavenly visions.

CHAPTER 44. THE SPIRIT OF PROPHECY IN AELRED

Hence also, as some do testify, he was made worthy of the spirit of prophecy, by which on occasion he ordered certain of the brethren to confess their sins before they had confessed and told them of things which they had done in secret, with details of time and place, lest they should add to their perdition by shrinking from clear and oral confession to the father. O peerless man, to whom the Lord deigned to reveal the secrets of men! O what a fine and prudent shepherd was he to whom God the Shepherd of shepherds showed in the spirit the vices of the flock! O man after God's heart, endowed with the spirit of prophecy, in the correction of his sons, by that spirit of the prophets which blows where it wills and no man knows whence it came or whither it goes![120]

CHAPTER 45. THE DEVIL IN THE DORMITORY

In this time two monks shouted out by night in our dormitory, terrifying beyond measure. They bellowed like bulls and aroused nearly the whole convent by their dreadful vociferation. Their clamor of terror echoed about the place in a reverberation of sound. They groaned and sighed wretchedly. In the morning someone told the abbot what had happened and made him aware of the fright which he had had in the night. To whom the father [said], 'Son, the devil truly came among the brethren there by night, trying to seduce one or other of them, but was forced to depart in utter confusion; his malice was in vain. Nevertheless, somebody gave way to him a little.'[121]

CHAPTER 46. A SERMON IN THE CHAPTER-HOUSE

About the same time, in chapter, in the course of a solemn and noble sermon, among other things he made this pronouncement: 'Brethren, look to your life, amend yourselves, set your minds upon your salvation, for I declare to you as a fact, that one of you has approached the Body of Christ to his damnation, and I know him; but I am not willing to name him, for I have his reformation at heart and I spare his blushes.' The brethren marvelled greatly, especially those who were conscious of some fault in themselves; and, when the sermon was ended, went to him and opened to him the secrets of their hearts.

CHAPTER 47. A MONK'S VISION OF AELRED DEAD

In the same time a certain religious brother had a vision in the night. He found himself in front of a high building of the most skilful construction, spacious and beautiful, with only one tiny access door. It had no window, opening, or lattice of any kind by which the place could be lit; the only light came from a sunbeam through the open door. The woodwork of the temple was sweet to smell; he was attracted by its fragrance to a nearer view, and the nearer he came the more he was delighted by the sweetness of its marvelous scent. When he reached the door and looked in he saw on the pavement a bed, and lying on the bed was his abbot, as though dead. When he saw this he could not withhold himself from entering, for he was greatly grieved by what had happened to his father. So he went in and came to the prostrate figure. The father showed no sign of life: he lay as dead, motionless, lifeless, breathing not at all. The brother wept freely at the sight and wailed, and, tearing the hairs of his head, gave way to piteous lamentation. While so engaged he lifted his eyes to the roof and saw the form of a man shining with a brightness greater than that of the sun, more than anything which carnal eyes can see in this world, so pure and clear, so undimmed did it glow in the fullness of its brightness. Just as trees and buildings and everything else that we can see gain splendor from the rays of the sun, so the whole edifice was resplendent in the light of that figure. It glistened and shone as though it had been lit by a thousand candles. The brother could see the other side of the figure through every part of it as clearly as if he had been there. The image appeared to float in the middle of the house without any hold or tie from above, or any support from below or aid to hold or constrain it in place from any side. It hung in the empty air like a globe of flame in cloud. Indeed, a tiny cloud could be descried near the navel of the image, dim in comparison with the rest, not adhering to its light but, as could be seen at moments, hanging from it.

While the venerable brother was gazing in his dream at the appearance in unspeakable astonishment, lo and behold a man of most pleasing countenance, dress and speech stood beside him and asked, 'What are you marvelling at? Why do you not gaze on your father who, as you suppose, lies dead before you rather than at that figure?' And he, 'Lord, the glory of that image made me forget the death of the very sweet father.' And the other said, 'Say not so; your father is not dead; for this figure which you see is his soul.' The brother, 'O my lord, do not lie to me, I beg.' 'Far be it from me,' he said, 'I speak truly. This image is the soul of the abbot of Rievaulx.' And he, 'Whose?' The other, 'He who is named Aelred, whom you see lying in this bed.' The monk, 'Do the souls of the just shine like this?' 'Even so,' said he, 'as it is written, The righteous shall shine forth as the sun in the Kingdom of their Father.'[122] The monk, 'Lord, what is that tiny cloud moving about the navel of the image; what does it there?' 'Only that,' replied the other, 'only that among the deeds of your abbot has still to be changed into light, and when it is he will go to God. He cannot die before that tiny cloud is taken away and his soul is cleared of this reproach. And that you may know that this pure image is his soul, shining as you see, behold it enter his body, and then it will be as it used to be.' In the flash of an eye, as he spoke these words, that glittering figure slid through its mouth into the body of the recumbent father, and immediately the monk saw the abbot stir as though he would rise from the bed on which he lay. The brother, overcome by the newness[123] of such great joy, called out so loudly that the monks resting in the dormitory were forced to rouse him. Now we have written this down because this same brother, who saw these things, is to be believed as a man of unstained life and well known and attested,[124] and as one worthy to see the truth even in his sleep, especially the truth about a father of such great sanctity.

AELRED'S SUFFERINGS DURING THE LAST YEAR OF HIS LIFE

Throughout the last year of his life a dry cough racked his chest and, added to all his other various infirmities, so weakened and wearied him that sometimes, when he came back to his cell after Mass in the church, he could for an hour neither speak nor move but lay as though unconscious on his pallet. The cough was due not to the flow of rheum but to the hoarseness caused by an intense dryness and stringency from the pit of the stomach to the top of the throat. It broke and impeded the normal course of his vital breath and, so to speak, almost prevented the passage of life to and from the heart, so that what little breath he could take and give out went, as it were, by a secret passage, through his nostrils. A feverishness which, starting from the brain, affected the sockets of his eyes, forehead and every part of his head was so great that he could not endure for an instant, because of the pain, the weight of anything placed upon him, from the crown of his head to his extremities. Indeed, in my opinion, the suffering in his breast and the difficulty of breathing were all due to an abnormal distemper in the head, producing fresh fever, and this in turn, when his body was racked by the cough, set up irritation together with the coughing. For he felt a weight on his chest, his tongue was rough, his gullet ulcerated and contracted, his jaws burning with great thirst.[125] As has been said, he endured this suffering for a whole year, until on Christmas Eve, when bodily pain tormented him more than ever and his illness harassed his life here on earth, he began in his turn, in his strong and unconquerable soul, 'to depart and be with Christ.'[126] Wherefore he said, 'Brethren, to be with Christ is by far the best. How much longer shall I be able to endure this dreadful trouble of the flesh? I wish and crave, if it please him, that God may speedily deliver me from this prison and lead me into a place of refreshment,[127] to be with him in the place of his marvelous tabernacle.'[128] The brethren, hearing these things, for he was speaking in chapter, hearing, I say, these things, began to sigh and weep. Whence came their sighs, whence their tears? Because, without a doubt, they saw that the infirmity and the will of the father were at one, and by this they, his sons, came to know that he would go away from them altogether. That day, after he had edified them greatly by his witness to the divine word, he went back to his cell.

CHAPTER 49. AELRED'S LAST DAYS

He attended Vespers, and again, in the night, he was at Vigils,[129] and in the morning in the chapter-house he preached to us a sermon crowned with a proem of deep humility, delivered from the heart to the heart, and with much fatigue of body. He was present at Mass and also at Vespers when he sat by the steps of the presbytery. After Vespers he was received into his cell and laid on his bed by the hands of his servants. For two hours he lay as though unconscious and half dead; then I came and saw the father sweating in anguish, the pallor of his face flushed, his eyes filled with tears, the ball of his nostrils twitching, his lips bitten by his teeth. I said to a brother, 'Of a truth the lord abbot now suffers much, for those changes in his members are signs of great pain.' But he, gazing on me fondly—for he was so sweet—said, 'Yes, my son, yes, yes, just as you say; I am greatly vexed by the agonies of this sickness; by the will of the Lord Jesus there will soon be an end to all this trouble.' In that hour some of the brethren wished to talk with him about the business of the house and were standing around his bed. He asked me to tell them that he had not enough breath to frame his words and was too tired to do anything; which I did, and not without tears.[130] In the night and on the next day he felt somewhat easier, and when I came to him he looked at me cheerfully and said, 'Yesterday, my son, we were confused and could hardly speak and grieved much therefore, especially because we lacked words to comfort the brethren, as we did only two days ago.' But the following night brought the father great pain, and us most pain of all, for his was only of the body while ours was the pain of a sorrowful mind, exceeding sad because of him. And so he continued, very weak in flesh, yet very strong in spirit; from that night he gradually failed in body, although he always maintained his usual force of mind. As he lay in bed he talked constantly in gasps, and day by day his body got feebler, until at last on 3 January he ordered all the monks to be summoned to him, and made them this allocution:

CHAPTER 50. HIS ALLOCUTION TO THE MONKS

'Often I have begged your permission when I had to cross the sea, or it was my duty to hasten to some distant region, or I had occasion to seek the king's court; and now by your leave and with the help of your prayers I go hence, from exile to the fatherland, from darkness to light, from this evil world to God; for the time has come when he, who redeemed me of himself without me, and deigned by his grace to bind me more closely to himself in the bonds of a better life among you, will take me to himself. Let it suffice,' he went on, 'that we have lived so long, for we have a good Lord and now it pleases my soul to see his face. May he protect you always in the good and deliver you from all evil; may he who does not desert his saints and is blessed for evermore never forget you.' When they had responded 'Amen,' the most pious father added: 'I have lived with a good conscience among you, for as I lie here, as you see, at the point of death, my soul calls God to witness that, since I received this habit of religion, the malice, detraction or quarrel of no man has ever kindled any feeling in me against him which has been strong enough to last the day in the domicile of my heart.[131] I have always loved peace and the salvation of the brethren and inward quiet. By the grace of Christ I have commanded my spirit that no disturbance to the patience of my mind should survive the setting of the sun.' At these words we all wept, so that for tears one could scarce see his neighbor, and most of all when he, weeping, said to us, 'God who knows all things knows that I love you all as myself, and, as earnestly as a mother after her sons, "I long after you all in the bowels of Jesus Christ."'[132]

CHAPTER 51. HIS ADVICE ON THE CHOICE OF HIS SUCCESSOR

After this he ordered to be brought to him his glossed psalter and the *Confessions* of Augustine and the text of John's Gospel and the relics of certain saints and a little cross which had belonged to Henry, archbishop of York, of good memory,[133] and he said to us, 'Behold, I have kept these by me in my little oratory and have delighted in them to the utmost as I sat alone there in times of leisure. "Silver and gold have I none"[134]; hence I make no will, for I possess nothing of my own; whatever I have and I myself are yours.' He also admonished us in the choice of a successor to seek the things of God and not our own,[135] and that the younger should pay special heed to the judgement of the priors of the house and to the older and wiser in this matter.[136] Then he gave us his paternal blessing and sought the divine blessing.

CHAPTER 52. AELRED IS ANNOINTED BY ROGER OF BYLAND

On the following day[137] he was anointed with the holy oil by Roger, the venerable abbot of Byland,[138] and fortified by the viaticum of the most sacred mystery of the Body and Blood of Our Lord, he calling out with tears, 'Lord, I am not worthy that you should come under my roof'.[139] After this his face looked brighter and fuller, and all that day and the next until the second hour of the night his looks held the same animation. Yet no masticable food passed his lips from the tenth day until his death.

CHAPTER 53.

From the second hour of the second night after he had received the sacrament of the holy oil he began to fail in speech, and, as though he were already in heaven, to take less account of earthly things. Until the end his five senses were unimpaired, but the words which he spoke were very brief and broken. All of us came together in one, not doubting of the father's passing to God, and vying with each other in pious zeal in ministering to his needs in his weakness. There were now twelve, now twenty, now forty, now even a hundred monks about him; so vehemently was this lover of us all loved by us. Blessed is that abbot who deserves so to be loved by his own. And he indeed, whose memory is blessed forevermore, himself counted this the greatest of all blessings, that he should be chosen by God and men to be so well beloved.

CHAPTER 54. *FOR CRIST LUVE*

To wait by his bedside during those days was, I confess, an awe-inspiring experience, though it had its happier moments. It was awesome because, as I suppose, angels were conversing with him, but only he could hear them, and, unless I am mistaken, he was replying to them all the while; for we heard him say again and again, 'Hasten, hasten'; and often he drove the word home by calling on the name of Christ in English, a word of one syllable in this tongue and easier to utter, and in some ways sweeter to hear. He would say, and I give his own words, 'Hasten, *for crist luve,*' that is, 'For the love of Christ, hasten.' When I said to him 'What, lord?' he stretched out his hands, as to heaven, and, fixing his eyes like lamps of fire upon the cross which was held there before his face, said, 'Release me, let me go free to him, whom I see before me, the King of Glory. Why do you linger? What are you doing? What are you waiting for? Hasten, for the love of Christ, hasten.' I tell all of you who may read this that in all my life I have never been so stricken to the heart as I was by those words, so often repeated, so awfully uttered, by such a man at such an hour, by a good man at the point of death. And these words kept proceeding from his mouth through three whole days. For three days life lingered with slow gasps of breath. So strong was the spirit in his fragile body that, even though his body failed, he was scarce able to give way to death.

CHAPTER 55.

In this same time a brother of our society, one of the father's personal attendants, lay sleeping from weariness, and behold! the father, in his infirmity, appeared to him and said, 'Brother, when do you think that I shall depart?' He replied, 'Lord, I know not.' The father, 'My soul, the handmaid of the Lord, will migrate from the earthly home where it has dwelt until now, on the day before the Ides of January.' It happened exactly as the father had foretold to the sleeping brother; for the father left his body on the second day after the brother heard these things from the father.

CHAPTER 56.

On the day before he died the abbot of Fountains[140] and Roger, abbot of Byland, with nearly all the monks and several of the *conversi*, were with him. A brother was reading the story of Our Lord's Passion, and he was listening, no longer able to speak a word that could be understood. Yet whenever anything was recited of Our Lord's humility or of the faithfulness of the disciples, as he could not speak, he would show his praise and joy in the passage by motions of his hands, sometimes moving his lips in the likeness of a truly spiritual smile. At other places, where Peter denies or the Jews accuse or Pilate assents or the soldier crucifies, he wept and indicated with his fingers the cruelty of the act, and his whole countenance expressed sadness. As the reading proceeded you could see in all joy and grief running together, smiles and tears, the voice of exaltation and the sighs as from one mouth, at one time, the same in all and all in each, on communal procession. To rejoice with the father, to grieve with the father, was an act of piety, just as it is the part of a son to bewail the death of a father and also, as he is still a father, to rejoice with him in his happy release.

CHAPTER 57. AELRED'S DEATH

I sat with him on that day and held his head in my hands, the rest sitting apart with us. I said to him in a low voice, so that nobody would notice us, 'Lord, gaze on the cross; let your eye be where your heart is.' And immediately raising his eyelids and turning his pupils to the figure of truth depicted on the wood, he said to him who suffered death for us upon the tree, 'You are my God and my Lord, You are my refuge and my Saviour. You are my glory and my hope for evermore. Into your hands I commend my spirit.'[141] He uttered these words clearly as they are written, although for two days he had not spoken so many words, nor afterwards did he speak three words together. Indeed, in the very next night his breathing was slower than before. So he lay until close on the fourth watch.[142] Then, when we were aware that death was near, he was placed, as the monastic custom is, on a hair-cloth[143] strewn with ashes, and, as the brethren with the four abbots who were there gathered about him, he surrendered his spotless spirit into the hands of his Father, and was at rest in Christ. He died about the fourth watch of the night before the Ides of January, in the year of the Incarnation one thousand and sixty-six, which was the fifty-seventh year of his life.[144]

CHAPTER 58.

When his body was laid naked before us to be washed, we saw how the glory to come had been revealed in the father. His flesh was clearer than glass, whiter than snow, as though his members were those of a boy five years old, without a trace of stain, but altogether sweet, and composed and pleasant. There was no loss of hair to make him bald, his long illness had caused no distortion, fasting no pallor, tears had not bleared his eyes. Perfect in every part of his body, the dead father shone like a carbuncle, was fragrant as incense, pure and immaculate in the radiance of his flesh as a child.[145] I was not able to restrain the kisses which I gave his feet, though I chose his feet lest affection rather than love should reproach me; the beauty of one who sleeps rather than delight in one who lies as he lay. Whenever I think of him then, I am still overcome by joy and wonder at the gracious recollection. And when do I not think of it? When do I not brood on that sweetness, that beauty, that glory? My God! he did not die 'in darkness, as those that have been long dead,'[146] not so, Lord, but in your light, for in his light we see your light.

CHAPTER 59.

When his body had been baptized (not that it was necessary, for the water flowed from him more limpid than before, but because it is customary), when, then, that golden vessel had been baptized, someone brought to us in a vessel a little of the balsam which the father had had as medicine. With this liquid, or rather drop of liquid, for the vessel which held it was hardly larger than an almond, with this, I say, this drop, I held that three of the father's fingers should be anointed, the thumb, the first and the middle finger, because it was with these that he had written many things about God. Some, however, preferred the tongue, others the face, although there did not seem to be enough to anoint a single joint. But when the venerable abbot Roger of Byland had extracted from the vessel by means of a tiny piece of wood nearly all the ointment on to the tip of his thumb, he anointed the face of the father, forehead, ears, neck, eyes and nose and the whole of the head, and still there seemed as much left as when he began. We are all amazed at the abundance of the ointment, and, as we were marvelling, the abbot Roger proceeded to anoint the father's hands, and he anointed as freely as before—and still we discern no less balsam than before. In the end we perceived that much of the arms had also been sprinkled by the same; nor was the anointing ended, for the heavenly blessing of the plentiful infusion still hung on the abbot's fingers. But the convent of the brethren was waiting. We hastened to carry the father to them, and then at last the abundance of the balsam ceased.

CHAPTER 60.

Later the body was borne into the church, and on the morrow, after Mass had been celebrated and the rites of the father's funeral duly observed and brought to an end, he was taken for burial in the chapter-house next to his predecessor the venerable, saintly and first Abbot of Rievaulx, William, whom we have mentioned above, and with whom and for whose merits and the grace of the Saviour seen in him he will rejoice and be glad exceedingly, as is right, before God and Our Lord Jesus Christ, to whom be the glory for ever and ever. Amen

Here ends the life of the venerable Aelred, abbot of Rievaulx. Here begins the lamentation of the author of the same life concerning the same matter.[147]

LAMENT FOR AELRED

In the prologue, in the development, and at the conclusion of my lament—lest I appear ridiculous by supplying to authorities first a rationale and a descriptive picture of those things that I am offering in the report—I will attempt to expedite things, setting down a clear likeness by accurate assertion of the matter at hand, and I will then press home to you the truth. Thus I touch upon the elements of the dutiful work I have undertaken, that in pursuing the matter on behalf of those worthy of hearing it, they may be able to anticipate with some genuine understanding the concluding prayer, if so they wish. Thus therefore with the confession of a struggle brought to light in the published preface and the cause of my lament supported by rational conjecture, the reenforcement of respected authority may offset any conjecturable shortcomings.

I am not so carried away without the authority of truth in these points of sorrow that I should wish to hide who said what or quoted someone, for in the manner of arrangement the narrative may deceive, and a thing will not change in memory if its origin is not concealed. The subject of the following pages, then, is the death and passing of my friend, the grief of my mind, the witness of his end . . . ,[1] the end of his word, I say, the final cause for this lament of mine, that is, for the departure from life of my friend, a fellow sufferer for the Word, and my sorrow down to the very end.

The key point of my lament, I suggest, is now shortly to be brought forward, if in this inexplicable madness of my attachment I am not reduced to nothing. There is a twofold course of affection, alike not only in pleasure but also in sorrow. Already tears are urging my soul to go further. They say, 'What are you doing, Walter? Look, we are running, but why are you standing still? Tranquility of life does not slow us down, yet you hang back even now.'

I no longer say I will go with you and follow you wherever you lead. Let us now go along together. And look, in all this I see Aelred being taken from me into the clouds, and I cry out, 'My father, my father, the chariot of Israel and his charioteer!'[2] O tears, where are you? 'We will run after him', they say. And, they say, 'Lament, Walter, lament, for your prophet has left you; your father and lord has been taken up on high.' For this I must lament and grieve and mourn for the prophet, for my father, for my lord. I mourn and I lament deeply. I am incomparably, unspeakably afflicted with grief, because the clouds have now taken him from my view and he has fled from my sight. O tears, I shall content you with the plaint of my voice, seek to furnish a testimony that you may see how such a man, so kind, so sweet, is adequately lamented. I am speaking of general, common, spiritual laments; I say, I am speaking of universal as well as particular lamentations. Like the Song of Songs, like middling and simple songs, so I know are the best, the mediocre, and the worst [songs]. These last are mine, for I grieve not for what has happened in itself, but instead for the misfortune to me of what has happened. And although I myself may be a physician by profession, still I apply treatment not without sharp grief. But the assured cure of this art makes clear what depends on medicine apart from the body.

This is my weakness, and very great feebleness, that a spirit of the quality of the spirit of Aelred, abbot of Rievaulx, left his body. My sorrow stems not from this. I do not grieve that his soul, worthy under God, has ascended to the Creator. Then why?

Because life has deserted me, that spirit of my life by which my spirit was living well.[3]

O tears, I speak to you. 'We hear,' they say, 'and at once abide with you.' I confess that I find no remedy save in one alone, save in him in whom I may live well. This one medical remedy prepares the outcome. To grieve for what is good multiples the increase of evil . . . [4] for the sufferer. I grieve, in fact, because as a physician [I cannot provide] medicine for myself. My physician was my abbot. Who? Aelred—someone than whom there is nothing sweeter, nothing more effective, nothing more curative for my illness. How? He was equal in soul as well as in body to many a great [saint].

O Lord Jesus, who will give me the wings of a dove that I may fly to him and be healed?[5] He has set out on a journey to a distant land and will not return for a very long time. I am left here, homeless and rootless, thrashing about in quicksand. Because I am sure of my weakness and unsure of my health, I grieve much more because the physician is gone by whose medicine I was living well. Woe is me, my lord [abbot]. Who will let me die for you who lived so usefully for me? And is it not so for others as well? Indeed, for very many others, for your God made you a father to many. And what kind of father? Primarily kind, full of good will, chaste, sober, discerning in prudence, humble, peace making, pleasant in charity, good at dispelling harm and all sorts of weaknesses from every brave soul, knowledgeable in healing, and provident and skilful in preserving health. Did any sick person appeal to Aelred and not immediately sense his healing gifts? An eminent sophist with a barrage of words and a flood of emotional speech reveals maladies of minds. This education in charity was so close to us that it approached the richness of a mother's milk for her sons and undeviatingly displayed the grace of a responsible father.

Great patience, present within and without, built a bridge over the waters of human malice and yielded to no gratification or adversity that might in any way bring danger on himself or on his own. He so shared the generosity of his spirit that with him, before the abundance of his substance failed, the liberality of his heart, according to his own derivation of his name, always gave preference to the dative over the vocative.

Are you streaming down, my tears, or not? 'We are streaming, Walter. We are streaming down, and we want you to suffer with us.' I am suffering, bearing the burden for you, for I begot you in grief. Little by little, quite calmly, my tears, wash and restrain the blow until the time of the real flood, lest turbulant wastewater overcloud the serenity of his word, and this lament interrupt his voice.

You know that music is an unsuitable accompaniment to grief. And you realize equally well that the waters of Siloam flow in silence.[6] Therefore I irrigate with a rivulet rather than with rapids. Lay out a straight water course, but I will stick my finger in it and force you to retreat until you are invited to return. Popular opinion declares tears shameful and mocks the strong for the flood. Spare me then, at least on this point. Hear me now in this stunned silence, and I will whisper the truth to your listening ears.

How easily, in fact, how much more easily is the past buried than a lifeless body. Eternal time is nothing today when the corpse is to be buried in the grave today. Anything may happen by the time it is changed for the worse.

Where then is our Aelred? If we ask the years and months and days and hours of his past life, they have all passed away like a shadow.[7] They are no longer here. Yet what was not buried is still not buried but burned away as if it were nothing. Even the fool knows that to ask where nothing is is meaningless. Therefore I will not ask this, but I will ask where Aelred is. Whom should I ask? It is not my tears, blinding my eyes, that prevent me from seeing him, even if he could be found. Reason resists the confused reasoning of this question in the meaninglessness of tears, however called up. Reason hates what is meaningless. I shall discuss this then with reason. With my Reason I shall converse. Come, Reason, explain to me what you sense. Where is Aelred?

I am not asking about his body, which lies in a coffin in consecrated ground, but about the life by which that body lived, and lived as well as Aelred lived. A beast of burden lives what

I would call a commercial life, because when it quits the body, [that body] ceases to belong to it. A dying cow leave its body behind it, not so much its life as a life [not its own], what I called a commercial life, because once the cow is purchased, the buyer makes its life to be nothing. Yet there is reason to say where Aelred is, for I care much less about the life of cattle. I am asking about the man who sought me out, formed me, established me, cherished me, nourished me, taught me, and loved me.

Where is Aelred? Here, here. Reason did all these things, and much more, for me. Then tell me where [he is]. To this Reason seems to say to me, 'When you ask him where he is, Walter, [this man] whom you feel is so agreeable⁸ and necessary to you, and the person about whom you ask has died, you are inquiring where he has sent his soul once his body is lying in the grave. You want, if I am not deceived, to know that his soul has gone to a good and light-filled place. You offered a good, though gloomy, place to his body and to others. You have set this upon this rock, for I heard you say, before you spoke with your tears, that this soul, worthy under God, had ascended to the Creator. I think you forgot that you heard this from me, so that in saying these things you presume to question me about this very thing especially. But since, as a handmaid, I owe you obedience at least in good matters, I will demonstrate by subtle reasoning that it is true that you proved he is there by using me, and indeed rightly, Before I pursue the construction of this reasoning, I ask you to note your own fragility and with your tears weigh the feeble condition of human life, needy, moribund, and wretched. Meanwhile, extend your view to the grave and carefully regard your father—the chains by which he is bound in prison, how humbly he lies in the dust, how dry is face is, how pallid his skin, how is he laid out with his bones exposed on stones—and [consider] what great value there will be to you in this sight!

'Where now is that ever gentle face, once smiling on his own and comfortingly coaxing them along? Where are the eyes filled with responsibility and the lips suffused with the dew of blessing? Where are the pure hands by which he accomplished such good works and wrote such godly words? They are all lying withered and dead, covered with stone and constricted by a mass of earth. What is lovely there? What is left that the dust does not darken, the earth does not touch? His eyes see nothing, his ears hear nothing, his mouth says nothing, his hands do nothing. You have deserved this ruling from God, as [offspring of] Adam stealing fruit for a greedy bite. There you hear, "dust you are and unto dust shall you return" '.[9] You have handed down this decision, this penalty, through our ancestors right down to us.

Therefore, thus lies abbot Aelred. If only my Walter lay like this, so that he [could ask], O Reason, what do you say of him? Do not curse your Walter. Reason says that it will be a blessing to you and I hope it will be the same to me. 'Where is your father's soul? Did you ask this of me, to be shown where he is? Without a doubt he is at rest, in light, in peace, and in the glory of God's grace. So is it written: "I will lie down in peace and take my rest".[10] This is the voice of just and disciplined[11] saints. He certainly is saintly, just, disciplined, and therefore in his sleep, that is, in his death, he has found peace and rest, for his body received burial in peace and his soul has passed to eternal rest. He has passed from light into light, from the light of the world to the lustre of Paradise, from mortal life to everlasting life, from the changeableness of the world to the stillness of heaven. Why then are you grieving, Walter?'

I am grieving, Reason, because my leader has abandoned me, submerged in a swamp of shortcomings, because my physician has left me gravely wounded and at the same time sick with a chronic fever, because the nourisher of my soul, leaving me sitting in the byways of vanity and ignorance, has hidden himself in a deep, remote place wholly inaccessible to me.

Reason says, 'You really are a man of small mind, and you pettily presume much of me. Why are you depressed? Why are you torturing youself? Why do you exhaust yourself shadowboxing? Your Aelred has paid the debt of the unspeakable transaction. He has entered the way of all flesh, because all persons die equally, or else they are not all mortal. How do all mortals exist? The prophet says, "What person lives and does not see death?"[12] Really, my dear Walter, in my opinion you should rejoice in the sleep of

a good man; otherwise you will seem by protracted lamentation
to blame rather than praise the person who has departed. If you
insist on conjuring up laments for your own sake, do it briefly,
or people will believe you love yourself too much. Are not all
laments raised to praise either those for whom they are made or
those who made them? You have read David's lament for Saul;[13]
you have read how he wept bitterly over the thankless Absalom in
a woeful lament,[14] yet Saul was considered unworthy of any sort
of burial and Absalom not only resisted heaven but was detested
on earth. You have read how the Egyptians lamented the death
of Jacob[15] and no less have you read in Ezekiel how the foolish
women bewailed Adonis.[16] But what is the value of these laments?
Lamentation is therefore not the best course; instead to live well
is best. Wherefore, dear Walter, live well and do not cut yourself
off from your Aelred when you someday come to take off the
clothing of mortality with which you are enclosed.'

With good conscience, Reason, have I often followed your
attachments, your wisdom, and above all, have I pursued these
delights by choice. Ought I in this fellow-suffering to lack patience
in adversity? 'No,' says Reason, 'but while the sorrowing mind
will be caught up in excessive agitation for a long time, moderation dictates that in such things eventually there are certain
bounds. As wine steadily drunk sometimes begets apostasy, so
water continually sipped creates internal ulcers. Since you have
been guided by me throughout the Life of your father, which
we have accomplished together in writing without emotion, it
behooves you to act this way now. In the prologue to this work you
excluded the impudence of emotion and promised that you would
enter briefly and wholly, as far as possible, into the description of
what had happened, admonished by me and instructed by my
learning.'

I do indeed want to be brought back to moderation.

'Here then I will end your lament with a prayer, begging God
to make you happy in the future, in the company and in the sight
of your beloved Aelred. May you, with me, reply together, Amen.'

WALTER DANIEL'S LETTER
TO MAURICE[1]

TO HIS FATHER and lord Maurice, outstanding in sanctity, Walter Daniel in sincere and devoted affection. As I seek to be brief, I am not going to wander into prolixity, although the two prelates who strive to becloud what I have done in the mists of uncertainty, and use the force of their authority to cast it into the pit of their suspicion and besmirch it as untrustworthy, compel me to write at some length. Far be it from your son, who knows that without truth there is no salvation, that he should knowinlgy allow himself to be branded as a liar. To come to the point, you enjoin me, lord, to insert the names of the witnesses upon whom I relied in the account of the miracles which I have described with God as my helper in the *Life* of our father Aelred, the venerable abbot of Rivaulx, and to do this for the sake both of the simple-minded folk who accept no big news unless many tell it, and of the unbelievers who mock at the truth, and also, if I am not mistaken, of those two prelates who, when you read these miracles to them, were unwilling to believe them, although it should have sufficed to clear me in the eyes of all men that in the course of the work I asserted that I had published nothing which I had not seen or heard, and that I had omitted very many fine things which I had confirmed by the verbal testimony of saintly monks. My will strives to obey your express wishes, my feelings engage and charity conforms me to be at the service of your command; and although in the body of the book which comprises the father's *Life* I deliberately cut short the testimonies of trustworthy men, I will bring them together in this letter, starting or rather following up with other of the more excellent miracles. Since only a few authors[2] have made use of this kind of statement in their description of *Lives* of the fathers and given the particular names of their sources, and in my view there should be no difficulty in believing that men of good life are able to do what God wills, that little book of mine stands, by the counsel of my friends, as it was composed, the outcome of your command being transferred, as I have said, to the present page, so that you may refer to it any unbeliever and especially those who have thought fit to suspect me of mendacity.

To proceed in order, I shall give the witnesses to the first miracle in the book, then to the second and so on. Here are the witnesses to the first, relating to the novice who left the monastery and whom God in his mercy brought back through the father's prayers: Henry and Robert, both of Beverley, monks and priests; Ralph the deacon, called the Short, himself a well-proved monk, and many others. Moreover, the venerable father Aelred told me about this miracle, not as a miracle, because of his humility, but, because of my own deficiency, as a remarkable happening. Then come three very noble miracles, which, through him, the lord did while he was abbot of Revesby; these are supported by such witnesses as the lord Gospatric, our monk and priest, Henry the priest, Ralph Short and many others. The next is the father's vision in his sleep of the monk who would return on the morrow to the monastery gate and would die soon after between his hands; there are as many witnesses to this sign as there were brethren in attendance on the dying man, for the father told them about the vision before the monk died. I will mention only three by name, the lord Daniel my father, Geoffrey the sacristan, Henry of Beverley. After this miracle comes the one which by the grace of God restored health and speech to the brother with the bad stomachic complaint who was made dumb; the sufferer himself, who was healed through the father, is a witness to this—his name

is Benjamin—, also William Ruffus, monk and priest, and Martin
the deacon, my fellow-servant in the Lord and a very dear friend
of mine. The witnesses to the next miracle are Ralph of Rothwell,
priest and monk, Ralph Short and the lay–brother, our shepherd,
who through the merits of the father recovered speech after he
had been unable to speak for two days; for he himself testifies to
it and 'we know that his witness is true'.[3] His name is Argar. The
next miracle concerns the young man who, stricken by unbearable
internal pains and at death's door, steadily recovered after the
venerable man had touched and blessed him; I was there myself
and other brethren of ours with me, of whom I will take two
in testimony 'that in the mouth of two or three witnesses every
word' of ours 'may be established.'[4] One shall be Arnold, at one
time our cellarer, the other Thomas of York, a young deacon of
good life and a son of holy conversation. I am unwilling to name
any witnesses to the next miracle for it is not expedient to do so; it
is possible that the abbot about whom that story is told did not die
for the reason for which it seems he died, although what occurred
happened as is written in the book.[5] The story which follows this
miracle, or, if you prefer, likeness of a miracle, currently stands—
the miracle of a man who swallowed a frog and was unnaturally
misshapen and disfigured, but was cured and delivered from the
danger of death through the venerable father. Reliable witnesses
to its authenticity are at hand, Robert our under-porter, a good
and excellent man, Henry of Beverley, Baldric the lay-brother,
who has been proved in many things, and almost more persons in
Galloway than can be numbered.

On all the other occasions which follow, I myself was present,
except that I did not see him rapt, 'whether in the body or out of
the body I know not,'[6] in mellifluous and indescribable visions.
He only told me privately that he had experienced sights of this
kind, so delightful and so sweet that, in comparison, he would
be entirely oblivious to everything pertaining to the flesh and pay
not the slightest heed to any temporal affairs. Let those believe
who will and let who will read, and let those who will do neither
reject both and despise what I, his son, have written about the
father. Only let them take heed that ignoble minds always breed

unworthy affectations and dismiss as false things sealed with the seal of truth—in other words, judge in a temper of injustice, not in the scales of inquiry with bias. The powers of belief in the hearts of the faithful might have been satisfied by my assertion that I have written only the things which I had seen or what others had seen and told me; but those two prelates accept nothing that is not attested by formal and public proof, as though crime and virtue are established by one and the same easy canons of faith, and this and that admit of an equal appreciation. Virtue is a form of light, discernible even to sleeping eyes by its own quality, but crime, as a figure of darkness, is shrouded in the colour of vice and cannot easily be seen; as it is written 'Who can understand his errors?'[7] Therefore, whoever rejects what is true, if what is preached bears the stamp of truth, shows that he himself is darkness, and does not recognize the image of the light when he hears it. For if he were light, he would recognize to be true what is part of the light, because like recognizes like, whereas the bad man defends the cause of the bad as his own. He finds it easier to believe that the splendour of light has put on the terror of darkness than that the light has maintained its true nature. How shameful, that prelates, heedless prelates, do not believe that the merits of a saint have given birth to miracles; as though the Father of lights cannot easily create what he wills in all things and Christ had not promised to those who marvelled at his works and believe: 'Greater works than these shall ye do.'[8] The man who does no good works does not believe, but those who do them do believe and cannot not believe in what is done. So it is through his conduct that a good or bad man receives or refuses faith. This is why bad men scoff at the things done by the good. Hence it is not to be wondered at if men of this kind hesitate to put faith in the virtues of our father. Indeed it is for you to resist those who stop their ears. Bring their rashness face to face, with the crowd of witnesses; show that it is not grace but sloth that hesitates. Tell them that 'a good understanding have all those who do his commandments.'[9] For as they do not create in themselves a good understanding they do not understand what is right. What is more right than to understand that the works of virtue are given by God to those who live soberly and piously and justly? Verily 'to him that has shall be given and he shall have abundance.'[10] It is very right that you, my father, you I say, for it is to you that I am speaking, believe me to have written only those things which I have seen and heard of my father,—and not all by any means, for I have omitted many well worth the telling. Here and now, in this letter, I will set down four of them, which I am sure will please you.

[1] The infant Aelred was lying in his cradle; a visitor, a man of remarkable grace, William son of Thole,[11] an archdeacon, comes to his father's house. He was a kinsman of Aelred and very fond of the child's father and mother. Entering the house, as I have said, where Aelred was lying in his cradle, he sees his face turned to the likeness of the sun, shining in dancing rays of splendour. It had gathered into itself so much light that when he put out his hand, it cast a shadow on the outer side while the outstretched palm, turned towards the infant's face, shone with the radiance of solar light, so that, as he looked at it, the serene countenance of the baby could be discerned gazing upon its own image perfectly reflected as in a mirror. The man marvels at the new sun which had risen in the house and tells the parents about the incomparable glory which he had seen in their child's face. They listen with joy and are happy in the thought that the shoots of felicity had sprouted in the soil of Aelred's infancy. They declare that one on whose earliest days such outstanding grace had smiled would in later life be a man of virtue. When he was old enough to understand it, his father, his mother, his brothers told him about it. I heard it from his own lips, and others heard it from him, Ralph of Rothwell, Henry of Beverley, Ralph Short and many more.

[2] Again, when he was a little boy he comes into the paternal abode from the games which little boys play with their fellows in places of public resort. His father looking upon him said, 'Well, my son, and what stories have you been hearing?' And he: 'Father, the archbishop of York died today.'[12] The man laughs to hear this, and all the family also, and commenting on Aelred's prophecy with whimsical politeness says, 'True, my son, he is dead who lives an evil life.' 'Not so, my father, in this case,' replied the boy, 'for on this day he has ceased to breathe and said goodbye to mortal

men.' Astounded at what they heard, they all wondered that the boy's mind should be concerned with such matters and give news of absent folk as though he were prophesying. They hope that there is something in the story of the prelate's death, so that their informant's report should have a basis of truth; but, as the place where the archbishop died was a long way off, the outcome of the prophecy hangs in doubt during that and the following day without any confirmation. On the third day, however, the rumor flies abroad throughout the province and the news of the pontiff's death becomes generally known. Then those who had laughed at the boy Aelred's prediction begin to weep and lament, not because he prophesied the event, but because the papa has died. Those who were aware of his prediction, as they talk together about Aelred, and all his sweetness, ask, 'What manner of child shall this be?[13] for the Lord revealed this to him.' And his father, in the fulness of his joy, treasured the things said about him and pondered them in his heart.[14] And after Aelred had become a monk, he was moved on a visit to Rievaulx to tell the delightful story to many of the brethren there. And our venerable father Aelred himself admitted to Ralph of Rothwell and Ralph Short and myself that he had heard it from his parents.

[3] Later, when he was in the guest-house at Rievaulx, the Lord deemed him worthy to work as follows through him. It was on the day before he was received into the cell of the novices. A big fire which was burning in that house emitted scorching balls of flame, first as far as the beams, then as far as the upper joists of the roof. The fire grew so strong in its fury that it was expected at any moment to destroy the top of the building. The abbey is filled with tearful lamentations, and a rapid concourse of *conversi*, monks, hired servants and guests strive incessantly to cope with the emergency, all using every means likely to be helpful in the disaster. Some were trying to subdue the greedy flames with water, some with wine, some with other liquids, but the greater their efforts to allay the burning heat by these means, the more the wet was consumed by the dry. At length, as the efforts of their strenuous measures are spent in vain, grief is joined by desperation. Now Aelred in that same hour was sitting with some

others at a table in the southern part of the house. Throughout the disturbance he had been unmoved in body and mind, but when one after another exclaimed, 'Woe to us, woe to us, there is no more hope,' with a smile of manly composure he took a tankard filled with native English drink from the table before him and, trusting in the Lord's mercy, lifted it and hurled the cider which the vessel contained into the midst of the flames, and, wonderful to say, they subsided on the instant and were extinguished as though the sea had flooded in. Oh, how the poor brothers exulted! Oh, the solemn praise to God, and thanks of praise to Aelred! The lord Gualo was there, and the incident affected him, also, so powerfully that to this day he cannot forget the impression made by his astonishment. And as by means of the four miracles contained in this letter I wish to suggest that our Aelred gave signs of his virtue in all periods of his life,[15] and as in the miracle just described he put out a big fire, I beg your attention a little longer so that you may learn in what follows how he diverted the element of water from its proper course.

[4] Two years before he migrated from the body, he was travelling in Galloway and came to Dundrennan,[16] as the abbey which the brethren of Rievaulx built there is called, and he stayed there six or seven days.[17] Since the natives in those parts live in pastoral huts and mean hovels, not in houses or foursquare buildings, and the abbey had only begun to build its regular offices[18] a short time before, they lodged the lord abbot and his brethren very attentively in a small dwelling. The servants spread the father's bed-clothes in a corner of the room and, so that he could rest quietly, made his bed as carefully as they could. As, whenever the slightest rain fell, it would wet the floor through some undetected channel, the brethren feared that this nuisance might cause the venerable man undue inconvenience, for no part of the roof, not even for the space of a couple of feet, was free from the penetration of the rain. But from the time when Aelred slept there the downpour was kept back from its usual depredations and although heavy rain fell almost continuously throughout those six days and poured through great holes in the crazy roof over the sleeping places of all the others who were resting with him in that

den, never in all that time is a single drop known to have fallen
on the father's bed. After observing this the provost and other
brethren of the church were amazed beyond belief, and attributed
to nothing else than to a saintliness in the man most pleasing to
God, that so fluid and unstable an element as water, so heavy in
its liquidity be so oblivious to its own nature as to withhold its
wonted course and twist and turn aside from the empty spaces
stretched beneath it.[19] As though to make it quite sure that this
novel and remarkable departure from the normal was all intended
to commend the merits of Aelred and to remove all doubts from
that time onwards in the hearts of the brethren that the drying
of that particular spot and of that alone was done to his glory,
after the father's bedding was taken away and it rained, the rotted
and leaky thatch let loose the usual harmful downpour[20] upon the
place where Aelred had slept just as it did upon the rest of the
floor. The lord Walter, our monk and sacristan, formerly Walter
Espec's chaplain, provides adequate testimony to the truth of this
pleasant miracle, for at the time when this incident occurred in
Galloway, he was prior of the house of Dundrennan, and often
tells the story of what he saw. In Oger, a son of Rievaulx and
a most reliable witness, we have another who testifies to it. I
will name a third, Henry of Beverley, a man as truthful as he
is lovable.

     Well, here you have a letter, laden with matter but not finely
wrought with eloquence, neither golden nor gilded, but of iron
and covered with silver, bejewelled with miracles and confirmed
by the support of witnesses. Here I might well end; none the less
I shall attempt first a brief reply to my two friends who in their
simplicity have thought fit to rebuke me because I was pleased to
say that in the first flower of his youth our Aelred lived like a monk
in the court of the king of Scotland.[21] What ignorance they show
of the rules of rhetoric which, by the brightness of its colours,
lights up the face of art so pleasingly by conveying its meaning
under cover of various sorts of figure. For what is their case? It
is that, because in that same period of his life Aelred occasionally
deflowered his chastity I ought not to have compared a man of that
sort to a monk. But in that passage I was not referring to Aelred's

chastity, but to his humility. By the word 'monk' I commended this; wantonness was not in my mind. I did not refer to the darnel but called attention to the wheat. I kept silence about the vices and insinuated the virtues. When, I beg, is grain without husks? No one is free from stain, not even the infant a day old. There is a rhetorical figure called *intellectio*,[22] by which the whole is known from a small part or a part from the whole. When I applied the word monk to Aelred I was making use of this figure, attributing a part by means of the whole, calling him a monk not because he was completely chaste but because he was truly humble. Humility and chastity make the proper monk, and since a good monk never lacks humility and the whole is known from a small part and the rule of speech is not infringed but laudably observed in this mode of expression, I said well when I used the word monk to describe a humble man. Those friends of mine, therefore, have unjustly abused me. Then they say, 'In your book you describe the body of the dead Aelred as glowing like a carbuncle and smelling like incense.[23] You have not expressed yourself with sufficient caution.' On the contrary, I was quite in order, though a peasant or an ignorant man might think otherwise with some justification. Even a mole, though it has no eyes, shrinks in fear from the rays of the sun. My blind friends do not blush to offend against the light. Hyperbole (*superlatio*), indeed, is a form of speech which exceeds the truth with the object of making something greater or less. By this and other colours mother wisdom employs her skill on the picture of eloquence. The heathen writer who said 'Speech sweeter than honey poured from his mouth' is an example of this.[24] And again in our books 'Swifter than eagles, stronger than lions.'[25] Or again in the Life of Saint Martin 'purer than glass, whiter than milk.'[26] Oh, you dullards! These are not extraordinary expressions, but, on the contrary, are plainly commendable. They emphasize great matters, and annoy foolish critics. For what are the facts? Is it supposed that the dead body of Aelred did not shine when it was washed? It was a light to all of us who stood by. And how? Much more than if a carbuncle had been there. That its fragrance exceeded the smell of incense seemed so to us; all of us were sensible of it. And no wonder; for never before in life was that fair and seemly man habited in flesh so bright as when he lay in death. I say without a grain of falsehood that I never saw such bright flesh on any man, dead or alive. You must pardon me, therefore, if I magnified the incomparable, as it deserved, by using a permissible hyperbole. If you do not, the experts in rhetoric will publicly trounce your stupidity.

In the meanwhile I spare you and I spare them, my lord father Maurice, on your account, lest the prolixity of this letter should put too hard a strain on your attention and its long-drawn conclusion be burdensome in your ears. So I come back to you.

Hear gladly, for I will now speak briefly about the miracles of father Aelred. They are great miracles, as you well know. If they were not, nobody would show ill-will; for rivalry and jealousy are roused by fine and glorious, not by dim and insignificant things. Is it so? So it is: our father's are great miracles. But bad men can work miracles, even great miracles. True, but only good men have the perfect charity of Aelred: 'Though I have all faith,' says the Apostle, 'so that I could remove mountains, and have not charity, I am nothing.'[27] Who would not say that to remove mountains is a great miracle; yet without charity whatever a man may do goes for nothing, even though he can hang the mass of the terrestrial universe upon one finger. Charity is a fine thing, a lovable thing, a thing which never lacks the rewarding fruit of eternal graciousness. Aelred had this and just as the Apostle describes it: kind, long-suffering, not puffed up, doing no evil, seeking not her own[28] but the things of Chirst Jesus. I, wretch that I am, wear the habit of a monk, I am tonsured, I am cowled, and as such I speak. I say, assert, confirm, swear, I swear it by him who is very truth, Christ our Lord, I marvel at the charity of Aelred more than I should marvel if he had raised four men from the dead. My hearers may laugh, they may mock at my words, they may throw my letter in the fire, they may do as they please, I hold fast and hope I may hold fast to this, that Aelred's charity, 'out of a pure heart, and of a good conscience and of faith unfeigned',[29] exceeded every novelty of miracle. And that I may show in a short discussion how right I am in feeling this, listen, my father, while your son tells a little story in which charity is clearly exemplified.

Once, when the peacemaking Aelred was suffering from colic
and tortured by the stone, he was seated on an old mat, which was
stretched beside the hearth, and in his wretchedness rubbing his
painful limbs. His body, looking by the fire like a leaf of parchment, was so bent that his head seemed altogether lost between his
knees. Overcome by his grievous malady he was trying to soothe
the pain in the heat; you might believe that the tongue of the
flame was licking his little body as he rubbed. As he cowered,
now here, now there, I was sitting beside him, alone, very sad,
for 'my soul was cast down and disquieted me,'[30] not so much for
the sharp prompting of my own mind as because of the father's
discomfort. And, as we two sat alone in the house, behold a monk
entered, mad with rage, like an Epicurean,[31] a bovine creature of
criminal aspect, moving in the vilest disorder. He came to where
Aelred lay. Bellowing cruelly and gnashing his teeth he seized hold
of a side of the mat, with the father lying on it, tossed them both
up with all his might and hurled the father of at least a hundred
monks and five hundred laymen into the fire among the cinders,
shouting 'O, you wretch, now I am going to kill you, now I am
going to destroy you by a hard death. What are you doing, lying
here, you impostor, you useless silly fellow? You shall tell no more
of your lies, for now you are about to die.'

I was consumed by the sight, and not suffering the danger to
the father, rose in hot indignation against the bully and, eager to
turn the tables upon him once for all, took him hard by the beard.
The giant, after the assault on the father, hurled his great hulking
body upon me, but my spirit was roused and I withstood him
boldly and checked his malicious efforts. In the meantime some
of the monks appeared and found the man, like a wolf standing
over a sheep, or rather, the shepherd, straining to get at him to
tear him with his teeth and devour him in his cruel jaws. They
also were consumed by what they saw and, in their burning zeal,
would have laid their hands upon the son of pestilence, had not
the father, heedless of his infirmity and mindful only of the call
of charity, bade them desist: 'No, no, I beg; no, my sons, do not
strip your father of the vesture of suffering. I am quite all right,
I am not hurt, I am not upset; this son of mine who threw me

into the fire, has cleansed, not destroyed me. He is my son, but he is ill. I am indeed not sound of body, but he in his sickness has made me sound in soul, for blessed are the peacemakers, for they shall be called the sons of God.'[32] And then, taking his head in his hands, the most blessed man kisses him, blesses and embraces him, and gently sought to soothe his senseless anger against himself, just as though he himself felt no pain from his own sickness and had been touched by no sadness because of the injury done to him.

Oh, the charity of the man, greater than many miracles. He did not order him to be expelled from the monastery, or beaten or bound or fettered as a madman; he would not suffer anybody to approach him with a chiding word. 'It was,' he said, 'against my person that he sinned, and I, when I wish, will revenge myself, but I never shall; for the charity of your father is not to be destroyed but rather perfected continuously until the end by such happenings as these, and it is in this way that we shall be saved.' When, where, to whom does such perfect charity as this bring no pleasure, a charity which, though so grievously exasperated by an inferior, renders no account, but on the contrary repays mad folly with kindness, surely the most perfect pledge of love. Read this, I beg you, my father Maurice, to those two prelates that they may know that the miracles wrought by Aelred, who brought forth such fruits in charity, were grounded in his merits, and that he, who showed himself so benign to the brethren subject to him, did his acts of virtue by natural right. In very truth, he, that fine maker of scarlet, most decorously adorned the form of his life within with a hundred times as many examples, and as many more, of this kind.[33]

I have placed this letter separately at the beginning of my little book so that reference may be made to it, as to a list of contents, especially when there is occasion to quote by name the witnesses to the incidents described. Pray for me, my father.

THE LIFE OF AELRED

1. Abbot H. has not been identified. It may be Hugh, abbot of Revesby after 1166.

2. Cf. 1 Kings 15:22 (VULGATE) = 1 Sm 15:22 AV.

3. Life falls into four stages in medieval writers: boyhood (*pueritia*), youth (*adolescentia*), manhood (*iuventus*), elderliness (*senectus*).

4. Ps 36: 27 (V)

5. See below, Chapter 32. The *Genealogy of the Kings of England* contains a eulogy for King David, who died on 24 May 1153.

6. Mt 5:.44; 1 Cor 9: 22

7. In Anglo-Saxon glossaries *disc-thegn* and *economus* are equated, as is 'stiward,' but this last word was not in common use before the eleventh century. After the Norman Conquest the English 'steward' became the equivalent, like the literary *economus*, of the *dapifer* or seneschal (*senescallus*). Cf. *Dialogus de Scaccario*, 2.19 : *per manum generalis economi, quem vulgo 'senescallum' dicunt* (Nelson's Medieval Classics, p. 116; Oxford edition, 1902, p. 151). See also L. M. Larson, *The King's Household in England before the Norman Conquest* (Madison, 1904), pp. 133–5.

8. Cf. Is 13:12

9. 1 Cor 15:10

10. *Triclinium*, equated with the Anglo-Saxon *gereord-hus* or hall.

11. This phrase (*quasi monachus*) aroused the particular reprehension of the two critical prelates to whom Walter Daniel replies in his letter to Maurice (below, p. 147 and note). Walter may have taken the phrase from the life of Saint Martin of Tours by Sulpicius Severus. *Vita Martini* 2.7: *triennium fere ante baptismum in armis fuit . . . ut iam illo tempore non miles sed monachus putaretur.*

12. 1 Cor 6:13

13. A play on Ps 57:6 (V): *vocem incantantium et venefici incantantis sapienter*

14. King David of Scotland.

15. Lk 14:10

16. If this description of the exaltation of Aelred's former enemy can be taken literally, he may have been the baron, Walter fitzAlan, who was to succeed Aelred as the first hereditary steward.

17. Ps 117:15 (V.): *vox exultationis et salutis in tabernaculis justorum.*

18. Walter Daniel uses the conceit of a soothing medicine, taken in this case to quiet the operation, not of a fever, but of a restorative cure (*remedium*).

19. Thurston (archbishop 1114–1140) actively supported the reform of monastic and canonical life in his archdiocese as zealously as he resisted the authority of Canterbury there. He had been in the papal party when Calixtus II in 1119 approved the constitutions of the Order and had supported the reform-minded monks of St Mary's, York, when they left their benedictine house to embrace the stricter cistercian life. He gave them the land on which Fountains Abbey would be built and supported them while they negotiated for entry

into the Cistercians. The foundation of Rievaulx was made 'with Thurstan's advice and approval' on 5 March 1132, according to the Cartulary of Rievaulx (*Cartularium de Rievalle*, Surtees Society [1889] p. 21). See D. Nicholl, *Thurston, Archbishop of York* (York 1964), and Aelred Squire, *Aelred of Rievaulx. A Study* (London 1969/Kalamazoo 1981) 15–19.

20. This friend might have been Waldef, established by this time as prior of Kirkham, or Thurstan, whom Aelred was visiting at the time, or some quite unknown 'close friend'.

21. The Latin *coturnix* is used in the Vulgate for the word translated in the King James Version as 'quail', but Walter, while remembering the quails in the wilderness (Ex 17:13), may well have had in mind the more familiar flock of white gulls.

22. Cf. Bernard of Clairvaux, SC 68.6: '*perniciosa paupertas, penuria meritorum.*'

23. Sg 6:3

24. Ws 11:21: *omnia in mensura et numero et pondere disposuisti.*

25. *Emina* or *hemina*, a measure of liquid. See RB 40.3.

26. Most of this passage is derived from the Rule of Saint Benedict or the Cistercian constitutions. It may be compared with Aelred's description in the *Mirror of Charity* III.35 (PL 195: 559–60; CF 17:279–287) . In one of his *Centum Sententiae* (no. 97) Walter Daniel wrote, in more general terms, another eulogy of the Cistercian rule. It contains the following passage: *Sicut enim color albus pre ceteris coloribus naturali quadam uenustate oculos mulcet intuentium, ita ordo cisterciensis pre ceteris professionum sectis, pictura quadam egregia et spirituali, omnes in se recapitulat virtutes in quo si quid minus habetur, hoc earum chatalogo certum est omnino deesse.*' (John Rylands Library, Latin {MSS 196, pp. 37ᵛ–38ʳ).

27. Ac 4:32

28. Rie Valley = Rye Valley.

29. Walter Daniel probably had in mind the passage in the letter of Saint Bernard prefixed to *The Mirror of Charity* [CF 17:70–71], but whereas Bernard was concerned to show how a region of rocks and hills and deep valleys can be transformed by spiritual blessings, this lyrical rhapsody reveals a delight in natural beauty which is Walter's own.

30. Cf. Ezek 11:19: *et auferam cor lapideum de carne eorum et dabo eis cor carneum.*

31. For the days of waiting in preliminary probation, see RB 58.1–5.

32. *probatorium*, the place of testing.

33. Aelred's novice master, later abbot of Wardon, or Sartis (*de essartis*, the clearing), in Bedfordshire. He was still living when Walter wrote. If he was abbot from the foundation of Wardon (1135), Aelred must have entered Rievaulx in 1133–34. See William Dugdale, *Monasticon anglicanum* 5:370, 522; 6:950; Jocelin of Furness in *AA SS* August 1:261b; G.H. Fowler, *The Cartulary of the Cistercian Abbey of Wardon* (1931) 357, and charters number 10, 12, 324.

34. Cf. Ph 3:14: *persequa ad brauium supernae vocationis Dei in Christo Jesu.*

35. Cf. Si 11:30: *ante mortem ne laudes nominem quemquam.*

36. Jn 15:13

37. Walter Daniel always refers to the abbey church as the *oratorium*, but, to avoid confusion with other oratories which are mentioned, I have translated the word as 'church'. It should be remembered that no permanent church could have been built by 1134, or for some time after Aelred joined the community. On the other hand, Walter Daniel says nothing about the remodelling of the chapter-house (with its apse unique in English Cistercian architecture), of work on the church, some of which survives in nave and transepts, or of the administrative buildings, all begun, if the archaeologists are right, in Aelred's time, and all, with the exception of the thirteenth-century refectory, kitchen and warming-house, still traceable, as late twelfth-century work, in the surviving ruins. See C.R. Peers in *The Antiquaries Journal*, 1 (1921) 272, and in *The Archaeological Journal*, 86 (1929) 21, 22. For the period of activity in Cistercian building on the abbey churches, see John Bilson's long paper in the *Archaeological Journal*, 66 (1909) 185–280.

38. RB 58.17–23, and the Cistercian constitution, in Ph. Guignard, *Les monuments primitifs de la règle cistercienne* (Dijon, 1878) p. 220.

39. 1 Sm 16:12

40. Ps 117:14 (V.)

41. Jm 1:17

42. 1 Cor 15:24, 28

43. Cf. Lk 12:5

44. Cf. 1 Sam 13:12 (= Vulgate 1 Kgs): *faciem Dei non placaui.*

45. Is 28:10: *modicum ibi, modicum ibi,* The AV reads 'Here a little, there a little.'

46. Bernard of Clairvaux, in his letter prefixed to *The Mirror of Charity*, refers to a description given by Aelred of his life at Rievaulx: *dicens te minus grammaticum, immo pene illitteratum, qui de coquinis, non de scolis ad heremum ueneris, ubi inter rupes et montes agrestis et rusticus victitans, pro diurna pane in securi desudas et malleo.* Cf. 2 Kgs 6:6 (4 Kgs V): *ubi magis discitur silere quam loqui, ubi sub habitu pauperum piscatorum coturnus non admittitur oratorum* (ed. A. Wilmart, *Revue d'Ascétique et Mystique*, 14 (1933) 389, 390, trans. CF 17:70).

47. Butter and honey: cf. Is 7:18, 22.

48. Ps 33:9 (V)

49. Ps 38:14(V)

50. William, first abbot of Rievaulx, was an Englishman and had been Saint Bernard's secretary before being picked to lead the foundation in Yorkshire. He died in 1145 (*Melrose Chronicle*, facsimile edition [London, 1936] p.34). The monks eventually placed his body in the wall of their chapter room where they venerated him (see below, chapter 49, note 29).

51. At the death of Archbishop Thurston in 1140, the canons of York

elected William, their treasurer, a nephew of King Stephen. The suspicion of simony led to a protracted appeal to the pope, led by the abbots of Rievaulx and Fountains and the prior of Kirkham, Aelred's friend Waldef. In 1142, Aelred was sent to Rome by Abbot William of Rievaulx to present the case against the not-yet consecrated archbishop elect. See John of Hexham in Raine, *Priory of Hexham* 1:133, 139, 142, and David Knowles, 'The Case of Saint William of York', *Cambridge Historical Journal* 5 (1936) 162–177, 212–214.

52. Cf. Is 52:4, and elsewhere

53. Adapted, as J. Dickinson has pointed out, from Saint Gregory the Great's description of Saint Benedict, *scienter nescius et sapienter indoctus* (PL 66:126).

54. Lk 2:48. In this passage, as in some others, Walter Daniel's abrupt transition from the past to the present tense has been disregarded.

55. The story is continued in chapters 21 and 28.

56. A new critical edition of the *Speculum caritatis*, made by C.H. Talbot, has been published in the Corpus Christianorum Series. An English translation by Elizabeth Connor OCSO appears in the Cistercian Fathers Series, volume 17 (1990). *The Mirror of Charity* was written at the encouragement, indeed the order, of Bernard of Clairvaux. Bernard's authorship of the prefatory letter was lost sight of for a number of years when it was erroneously and categorically ascribed to Gervase abbot of Louth Park, and was restored only in this century by André Wilmart ('L'instigateur du Speculum Caritatis d'Aelred abbé de Rievaulx', *Revue d'Ascétique et de Mystique* 14 [1933] 371–175) who gives due credit to T. E. Harvey, who discovered the attribution in a British Museum manuscript. In his introduction to the 1950 edition of this *Life*, Powicke (p. lvii) traces in some detail the error, which appears in such authoritative resources as Bertrand Tissier, *Bibliotheca Patrum Cisterciensium* (1662), J.-P. Migne, *Patrologia Latina* 195, and Charles de Visch, *Bibliotheca scriptorum ordinis Cisterciensium.*

57. 'Carried away as usual by his train of thought', Powicke comments, 'Walter suggests in his master a contempt for learning which was quite foreign to Ailred's mind.' He was well trained in grammar and had grown up in an atmosphere of intellectual interests. When he criticized curiosity and vain philosophy, ' . . . like St Bernard, he was attacking the moral dangers which beset the learned, not learning itself.' See his Introduction to the first edition, pp. lxxxvi-lxxxvii.

58. The two earlier daughter-foundations were Wardon (1135) and Melrose (founded 1136–37, but later moved to the present site.

59. Those were the days of the widespread disturbances in the reign of King Stephen. This passage provides the moral justification, in monastic eyes, for a territorial expansion which later aroused harsh criticism. Its outlook is confirmed by contemporary charter evidence, e.g. the arrangements by which Osbert de Wanci 'in the remote and wooded country between Banbury and Towcester,' provided 'against the lifting of his cattle and the capture of himself,

his wife and his son'; see F. M. Stenton, *The First Century of English Feudalism* (1932) 243–247, 284–285.

60. *Non erat sterlinis utriusque sexus:* literally, 'he was not sterile of either class,' i.e. either of the *officiales* or of the *claustrales*, typified respectively by Leah and Rachel. The twins of Leah are fear and justice, the twins of Rachel are prayer and love. The word *sexus* is used in the sense of class or condition.

61. Ps 33:10, 83:5 (V).

62. Lk 16:24: the cry of Dives in Hades.

63. Abbot William, at one time Bernard's secretary at Clairvaux, died on 2 August 1145. See the references and extracts in Raine, *Priory of Hexham*, 1:108–9.

64. Si 44:25.

65. See F.M. Powicke, 'Maurice of Rievaulx' in the *English Historical Review*, 36 (1921) 17–25. Maurice apparently entered Rievaulx very soon after its foundation in 1132, being already a distinguished Durham scholar. After retiring as abbot of Rievaulx, he lived in the community except for a few weeks as abbot of Fountains. A letter from a *pauper et modicus frater M mininius pauperum Christi de Rivalle* to Thomas Becket, identified by Powicke in this article as coming from the pen of Maurice, he later inclined to attribute to Aelred, who as abbot in 1163 would have been likelier to be corresponding with archbishops (Powicke, Introduction, pp. l–li)—ed.

66. Ps 115:15 (V)

67. Si 45: 2: *in uerbis suis monstra placauit*, of the Lord working through Moses.

68. Ps 73:23 (V)

69. Mt 11:19

70. 1 Tm 5:23

71. The quotation is from the translation of certain words in Ezek 34:3, 4, as given in RB 27.7, and differs from the version in the Vulgate.

72. 2 Cor 12:15

73. 2 Cor 12:10

74. The abbey of Swineshead, or Hoyland, Hoiland, in Lincolnshire was a daughter-house of Furness and had been founded by Robert Grelley. Like Furness and and other Savigniac houses, it joined the Cistercian Order in 1147, and would doubtless seek information on many matters from the centre of northern Cistercianism. Hence the mission sent by Aelred, soon after his election as abbot, to Swineshead.

75. 2 Cor 12:2.

76. Powicke was of the opinion that the monk, now stable enough to be trusted on an important mission, was bantering affectionately with Aelred.

77. Walter Daniel is not using the word *hospes* in a precise sense.

78. Consuetudines, ch. xciiii, in Guignard, *Les monuments primitifs*, pp. 206–7

79. Heb 12:14.

80. 1 Chr 29:15.

81. 2 Cor 1:12.

82. Ps 121:4 (V).

83. Ps 138:16 (V).

84. In *The Mirror of Charity* (PL 195: 563; CF 17:195) Aelred says that some three hundred persons were subject to the abbot of Rievaulx (1143). Here, twenty-five years later, the number is six hundred and forty, comprising *monachos, conuersos, laicos*. With these three classes of men compare the 'concourse of conversi, monks and hired servants (*mercenariorum*)' which tried to put out the fire in the guest house, referred to in Walter Daniel's letter to Maurice (below p. 152). The distinction between the laybrothers proper (*conversi*) and the hired servants or laymen connected with the monastery is formal, and was defined very clearly in one of the combined statutes issued by the General Chapter at Cîteaux in 1134 (*Statuta capitulorum generalium ordinis Cisterciensis ab anno 1116 ad annum 1786*, ed. J.M. Canivez [Louvain 1933–1941] 1:14): *Per conversos agenda sunt exercitia apud grangias, et per mercenarios quos utique conversos episcoporum licentia tamquam necessarios et coadjutores nostros, sub cura nostra sicut et monachos suscipimus et fratres et participes nostrorum tam spiritualium quam temporalium bonorum aeque ut monachos habemus*. In other words the hired servants were men, dispensed from episcopal authority, who shared with the monks and *conversi* the privileges of the monastic community. In 1187 Waverley Abbey had seventy monks and one hundred and twenty *conversi* (*Annales monastici*, ed. H. R. Luard [London 1864– 1869] 2:244). If this ratio held good at Rievaulx, the community there in 1167 would have comprised 140 monks, about 240 *conversi* and about 260 laymen or *mercenarii*. Again, the *conversi* were very clearly distinguished from the monks, as is seen in Walter Daniel's contrast between the contemplative and cloistered on the one hand and the *activi* on the other (above, chapter xx). I cannot accept Dom Wilmart's suggestion that the 140 monks at Rievaulx in 1167 included the *conversi* in a broad sense of the word *religiosi* (*Revue Bénédictine*, 37 [1925] 264, note).

85. Referring, as Knowles has pointed out (*Monastic Order in England*, p. 258), to Luke 24:28: *et ipse se finxit longius ire*, i.e. 'he used to pretend (*fingebat*) that he was hesitating about an applicant, so that he might appear to surrender against his will to the urgent prayers of the brethren.'

86. I have not found any other reference to this indulgence. It is perhaps worth noting that in 1157, when Walter Daniel's narrative suggests that it may have been issued, the Scottish abbots were granted the indulgence to attend the General Chapter every fourth year instead of every year (*Statuta*, ed. Canivez, 1:67). This statute shows that petitions from the northern daughter-houses of Rievaulx were presented in this year.

87. *Disciplinae* in the sense of observance of the monastic life, as frequently in the Rule of Saint Benedict.

88. Lk 22:26

89. Unless conditions changed rapidly after Aelred's death, Walter Daniel's

description of the happy unity in Rievaulx was idealized. Aelred's successor must have felt the need to tighten the discipline, so that defections were more frequent than in Aelred's time. See the papal mandate issued by Alexander III, some time between 1171 and 1181, to the parsons of churches in the province of York (*Cartularium de Rievalle*, Surtees Society (1889) p. 194, no. 261; and in Walther Holtzmann, *Papsturkunden in England* I, ii: 462). After referring to the harm which might be done to *regularis disciplina*, if the monastic vow could lightly be disregarded, the mandate proceeds: *Ideoque universitati uestre per apostolica scripta precipiendo mandamus et mandando precipimus, quatinus monachos uel conuersos monasterii Rieuallensis nullatenus recipiatis, sed potius, si deposito religionis habitu seculariter uixerunt, publice excommunicatos denuntietis et cautius euitetis et de parrochiis uestris penitus expellatis.*' This document must have been issued at the instance of the abbey.

90. Ps 120:4 (V)

91. Henry II, the junior to Henry I. The description shows that Walter Daniel was writing before the coronation in 1170 of Henry II's son Henry, who at that time, to distinguish him from his father, was known as the young King Henry. This 'Young King' died before his father. His coronation exacerbated the already tense relations between Archbishop Thomas Becket and King Henry II, and between Becket and the bishops who participated in the young king's coronation. According to Walter, Aelred was writing the *Genealogy of the Kings of England*, for the new King Henry II's benefit, when King David died on 24 May 1153.

92. Lk 2:42. *De Jesu puero duodenni*; CCCM 1:249–278; PL 184:849–870; translated by Theodore Berkeley OCSO, *Jesus at the Age of Twelve*, *Aelred of Rievaulx: Treatises and Pastoral Prayer*, CF 1:1–39.

93. Is 13:1. The sermons on Isaiah, written between 1158 and 1163, were published in 1163–1164 and dedicated to Bishop Gilbert Foliot. Aelred's Liturgical Sermons, edited by Gaetano Raciti OCSO, are available in CCCM 2A. A translation is in preparation.

94. *De amicitia spirituali*, CCCM 1:287–350; translated by M. Eugenia Laker SSND, *Spiritual Friendship*, CF 5 (1974).

95. *De institutione inclusarum*, ed. C.H. Talbot, *Analecta S.O.C.* 7 (1951) 167–217, and CCCM 1:637–682; ed. Charles Dumont ocso, Sources chrétiennes 76 (1961) 40–169; translated by Mary Paul McPherson OCSO, CF 2:43–102.

96. The Life of King Edward was composed in 1163, the year of the translation of the saint's remains (see next note). *The Life of King Edward the Confessor*, ed. Frank Barlow (London 1962); translation in preparation.

97. Lk 11:33

98. Laurence of Westminster energetically promoted the cause of the canonization of Edward the Confessor, whom Alexander III canonized in two bulls isued from Anagni on 7 February 1161. On 13 October 1163, the body of the saint was translated to a new shrine in the presence, perhaps, of Henry II

and an assemblage of Norman and English nobles, lay and ecclesiastical (Richard of Cirencester, *Speculum Historiale*, Rolls Series 2:319ff). The *Chronicon Anglie Petriburgense* (ed, J. A. Giles [London 1845], p. 96) claims that Aelred preached on this occasion, which seems unlikely.

99. *De anima*, edited by C.H. Talbot and first published in *Aelred of Rievaulx: De Anima*, Mediaeval and Renaissance Studies, Supplement I (London: The Warburg Institute, 1952) and subsequently in CCCM 1 (Turnhout: Brepols, 1971). Translation, by C.H. Talbot, in *Aelred of Rievaulx: Dialogue on the Soul*, CF 22 (1981).

100. The writer in the Bury MS (N.L. 2:551, ll. 36–42), in a summary survey, says that Aelred wrote more than twenty works (*opuscula*) in addition to one hundred sermons, the thirty-three homilies on the burdens in Isaiah, and three hundred letters.

101. Cf. Dan 2:45

102. That is, he took off his cowl and put on a hair-cloth over his under-garments. Or, he may have thrown off his cowl when he ran from the orchard. On the *cilicium*, see below, chapter 57, note 143.

103. This unidentified abbot seems to have been Philip of Revesby (died 1166). See Powicke, Introduction to the 1950 edition, pp. lxx and lxxx.

104. Prov 1:17

105. Cf. Hab 2:6: *aggravat contra se densum lutum*.

106. Although Walter Daniel was writing very soon after the events described in chapters 37–9, his chronology here is strangely confused. If, as seems most likely, the insolent abbot of a daughter-house referred to in c. 37 was Philip of Revesby, who died in 1166, Aelred could not have paid this visit to Galloway later in 1166 (though in fact he did visit Scotland in this year) and have returned from it four years before his death (1167) as is said in c. 39. Moreover, the resignation of Fergus of Galloway, his retirement to Holyrood and death, occurred in 1160–1, after the subjection of Galloway by King Malcolm in three campaigns (see the passages from the annals of Holyrood and Melrose quoted in Archibald Campbell Lawrie, *Annals of the Reigns of Malcolm and William* (1910) pp. 56, 67). Walter confused three visits which Aelred is known to have made to Scotland, in 1159, 1164–5, 1166.

107. Cf. Mt 8:20

108. Cf. Is 1:6: *a planta pedis usque ad uerticem non est in eo [Israel] sanitas*.

109. Dundrennan Abbey, said to have been founded by King David, *c.* 1142, but obviously later than Revesby in 1143 (see above, chapter 19, and Letter to Maurice, note 16). Revesby was the third daughter-house and Dundrennan the fourth.

110. Si 11:3

111. This peace did not last for more than six or seven years after the time of Walter Daniel's eulogy of the brothers. The two, Gilbert and Uchtred, revolted in August 1174 after the capture of William the Lion, king of Scotland, at Alnwick

in July. In September Gilbert murdered his brother. See William of Newburgh, in Richard Howlett, *Chronicles of Stephen, Henry II, Richard I* (London 1884–1889), 1:186–7.

112. I have slightly abbreviated this pathological extravaganza in translation.

113. Cf.Mt 8:2

114. Walter Daniel embroiders on this incident at such length that the influence of some widespread legend may be suspected, such as the Irish tradition of possession by a demon of hunger, of which traces can be found in England and Scotland throughout the centuries. The Rev'd Conor Martin has called my attention to the middle-Irish wonder tale, the vision of Mac Conglinne. See Kuno Meyer, *Aislinge Meic Conglinne*, with an introduction by Wilhelm Wollner (1892). In a Gaelic version a toad plays the part of demon. Walter Daniel's story differs from the Irish legend in two respects: the victim is not emaciated but swollen, and the frog is not induced to leave him by the provision of food.

115. The following chapters (41–8) are summarised in the *Sanctilogium* (N.L. 1:44–6). The Bury MS omits them.

116. Cf. 1 P 4:1

117. Ps 102:14 (V)

118. Jb 9:31

119. Ex 34:29 (V): *Et ignorabat quod cornuta est facies ex consortio sermonis Domini*; cf. also verses 30, 35. The A.V. reads: 'the skin of his face shone while he talked with him.'

120. Jn 3:8

121. On the moral problem created by the first involuntary movements leading to concupiscence, see Dom O. Lottin's study, with its collection of texts, in his *Psychologie et morale aux xiie et xiii siècles*, II, i (1948) 493–589. In one of his *questiones* on the subject, Stephen Langton refers to the monk in a reply to an objection: *Ita est quod, si primus motus duret usque ad a, erit peccatum mortale. In quolibet instanti ante a, tenetur reprimere et non reprimit; ergo peccat mortaliter ante a.* Langton replies: *Non ualet, quia non tenetur reprimere in aliquo instanti. Similiter monachus tenetur non pertransire hoc spatium; nulla tamen pertransitio erit ei peccatum mortale.* (Lottin, p. 510.)

122. Mt 13:43

123. Cf. Rm 7:6: *ut seruiamus in nouitate spiritus*

124. Cf. Deut 1:13: *quorum conuersatio sit probata in tribubus vestris*

125. This passage is obviously based upon close personal observation in-terpreted in the light of current theories. It may be compared with a passage in one of the visions in the *Liber Divinorum Operum Simplicis Hominis*, written between 1163 and 1170 by Hildegard of Bingen (1098–1179). An abbreviated translation of this passage (from Migne, PL 197:792–3) is found in Dr Charles Singer's essay on St Hildegard in his work *From Magic to Science* (1928) 224–6. For the obscure literary and medical background from which twelfth-century views on the structure of man, or the microcosm, derived, see Lynn Thorndike,

A History of Magic and Experimental Science during the First Thirteen Centuries of our Era (1923), especially chapters 31, 32, 40 (1:719–59; 2:124–54).See also, Peter Dronke, *Women Writers of the Middle Ages* (Cambridge 1984).

126. Ph 1:23

127. Ps 65:12 (V): *eduxisti nos in refrigerium*

128. Ps 41: 5 (V)

129. *Vigiliae*, the early morning office often referred to as Matins, which was the name then given to Lauds. See RB 8–11. 'Vigils' was also the name given to private and voluntary prayer, especially during the night, as, for example, when Waldef of Melrose, on a visit to Rievaulx, went into the chapter-house after Compline to pray by the tomb of Abbot William (Jocelin of Furness, *Vita Sancti Waldeni*, *AA SS* August 1:264e, 265a). For the injunctions to and practice of these vigils, see Ursmer Berlière, *L'ascèse bénédictine* (Maredsous, 1927) 205–10, especially the long quotation from Paul Warnefrid's eighth-century commentary on chapter four of the Rule of Saint Benedict.

130. This was Christmas Day 1166.

131. In the fifteenth century this passage, together with a short extract from one of Aelred's lost letters (no. 21), was added at the end of the abbot's pastoral prayer in the Rievaulx MS (now Jesus College, Cambridge, MS 34, f. 99) which contains it. This fact shows that Walter Daniel's work was in the monastic library and was still being read three hundred years after Aelred's death. See A. Wilmart, 'L'oraison pastorale de l'abbé Aelred' in *Revue Bénédictine*, 37 (1925) 271–2, reprinted in his *Auteurs Spirituels et Textes dévots* (1932).

132. Ph 1:8

133. Henry Murdac, the cistercian abbot of Fountains before his election to York.

134. Acts 3:6

135. Ph 2:21

136. According to the Rule of Saint Benedict, as observed by the Cistercians, *in abbatis ordinatione illa semper consideretur ratio: ut hic constituatur quem sibi omnis cohors congregationis secundum timorem Dei siue etiam pars quamvis parua congregationis saniori consilio elegerit* (Guignard, *Les monuments primitifs*, p. 51).

137. 5 January 1167 (n.s.)

138. Roger, abbot of Byland from *c.* 1146 to 1196, was elected abbot of his Savigniac community by acclamation, and was present at the Cistercian General Chapter of 1147, when Savigny affiliated its monasteries with the Cistercian Order. Roger led his community through its moves from Hood to Old Byland to Stocking and finally to New Byland, where the extensive abbey ruins can now be seen. See Lawrence S. Braceland, 'Introduction' *Gilbert of Hoyland 1: Sermons on the Song of Songs, 1*, CF 14:6–10.

139. Mt 8:8

140. Richard, abbot of Fountains from *c.* 1147 to 1170.

141. Lk 23:46

142. *Vigilia* is here used of a division of time, not as an Office. It is a watch in the night, between bedtime and Vigils/Matins. Monks, in the winter months, retired for the night about 6:30, so the fourth watch when Aelred died was about 10:30 pm on the day before the Ides of January, i.e. 12 January 1167 (n.s.). For the monastic *horarium* and method of reckoning the hours in winter and summer, see U. Berlière, *L'ascèse bénédictine*, pp. 51–4.

143. *Cilicium*; as also above (*c.* 48) when Aelred clad himself in one; it is a garment or cloth of skin, usually goat-skin, with the rough hairs unremoved. It was used for ascetic purposes next the skin, and, as here, at the time of death. See Ducange, *Glossarium mediae et infimae latinitatis* (1840), s.v. *cilicium*.

144. The Bury MS adds *et anno XX° postquam domum Rievallie suscepit regendum* (N.L., 2:552, l. 24).

145. In his defence of this passage against the strictures of the two prelates (below, Letter to Maurice), Walter Daniel himself revealed the model which he followed, the *Life of Saint Martin* by Sulpicius Severus: *Testatique nobis sunt qui affuerunt iam exanimi corpore glorificati hominis uidisse se gloriam. Vultus luce clarior renitebat, cum membra caetera ne tenuis quidem macula fuscaret. In aliis etiam et in illo tantum artubus non pudendis septennis quodammodo pueri gratia uidebatur. Quis istum unquam cilicio tectum, quis cineribus crederet inuolutum? Ita uitro purior, lacte candidior, iam in quadam futurae resurrectionis gloria et natura demutatae carnis ostensus est.* (Epistola 3.17.)

146. Ps 142:3 (V)

147. This colophon occurs in Jesus College, Cambridge, manuscript QB.7, f. 74r, written probably at Durham in the fourteenth century. Professor Powicke's translation ends here. Cistercian Publications expresses its gratitude to the Photography Department of Cambridge University, and to Dr Anna Kirkwood and Sr Jane Patricia Freeland for supplying, transcribing and translating this Lament within the extremely short timeframe allowed by its production schedule. When a critical edition of the Lament has been made, some obscurities and inaccuracies in the present translation can be corrected.

LAMENT FOR AELRED

1. The manuscript is defective at this point.
2. 2 K 2:12
3. *bene vivere*
4. Defective text
5. Cf Ps 55:6 ·
6. Cf Neh 3:15
7. Cf Qo 8:13
8. Text obscure
9. Gen 3:19
10. Ps 4:8
11. religious
12. Ps 89:48
13. 2 Sam 1:17
14. 2 Sam 18:33
15. Gen 50:3
16. Cf Ezek 8:14

LETTER TO MAURICE

1. Maurice may have been Aelred's predecessor, a learned monk who had moved from Durham to Rievaulx about 1138, was elected abbot when William died in 1145, and retired in 1147. A likelier candidate is Maurice, prior of Kirkham, a house of Austin canons. Powicke describes Maurice of Kirkham as 'an inquisitive man, full of fussy learning' and likely to 'have interested himself in the miracles of his former neighbour at Rievaulx' (Introduction to the 1950 edition, p. xxxi).

2. The practice of authenticating miracles by a list of witnesses was by no means new, and was frequently revived about this time in order to avoid or meet such criticism as that of which Walter Daniel complains. Cases in point are Jocelin's *Life of St Waldef* (*c.* 1200), and the various descriptions edited by James Raine in *The Historians of York* (1879), of the miracles wrought at the tomb of Saint John of Beverley. The most important and difficult example is that of Saint Bernard.

3. Jn 21:24

4. Mt 18:16

5. *Life*, chapter 37.

6. 2 Cor 12:2

7. Ps 18:13 (V)

8. Jn 15:12: *qui credit in me opera, quae ego facio, et ipse faciet et maiora horum faciet.*

9. Ps 110:10 (V)

10. Mt 25:29

11. For William son of Thole, an archdeacon in the church of York, see Charles Clay in the *Yorkshire Archaeological Journal*, 36 (1946) 284–5, correcting Powicke's earlier identification of him. When William son of Thole saw Aelred in his cradle he was not yet archdeacon. Walter Daniel wrote more than sixty years later, and naturally antedated the promotion of a well-known man. Mr Clay suggests that William son of Thole may have been identical with a William of Beverley, also famed as an archdeacon in the church of York in the middle of the century. For the archdeacons of Durham at this time see F. Barlow, *Durham Jurisdictional Peculiars* (Oxford, 1950) 153–6.

12. Thomas II, who died at Beverley 24 February 1114.

13. Lk 1:66

14. Lk 2:19

15. The writer is describing miracles from infancy, childhood, youth and age.

16. Dundrennan, in Dumfries and Galloway county, is thought to have been founded by King David I, perhaps with the collaboration of Fergus, Lord of Galloway. Its first abbot, Sylvanus, succeeded Aelred as abbot of Rievaulx.

17. Here Walter fixes the date as two years before Aelred's death. In the Life itself, he refers only to a visit made four years before he died. The date of at least one visitation is fixed by Aelred's presence at Kirkcudbright on Saint Cuthbert's day, 20 March 1164/65 (Reginald of Durham, *De admirandi Beati Cuthberti uirtutibus*, pp. 178–179).

18. According to the statute of 1134, buildings should have been ready for the monks when they arrived at the new foundation. See Canivez, *Statuta* l:15, and Guignard, cc. 12, 23, pp. 253, 256.

19. This type of miracle is common. For an even more startling story, see Jocelin's *Life of Saint Kentigern*, c. 35, ed. John Forbes, *The Historians of Scotland*, 5 (Edinburgh, 1874) 221.

20. Literally 'the separative backbending of dissipated straw did not cease to pour, in the usual way, harmful floods of water.'

21. See *Life*, chapter 2, note 11. For parallels in Jocelin's *Life of Waldef*, and in Aelred's own references to King David's son Henry, and Richard, prior of Hexham, see *AA SS* August 1:251e, and *Decem Scriptores*, col. 432; Howlett, *Chronicles of Stephen* 3:191, and Raine, *Priory of Hexham* 1:193.

22. The definition of *intellectio*, as also, later, of *superlatio*, is derived from the *Rhetorica ad Herennium*, ascribed to Cicero, iv, 33, 44. Bede defines the same rhetorical figure under the name *synecdoche*. *Synecdoche est significatio pleni intellectus capax, cum plus minusue pronuntiat; aut enim a parte totum ostendit,*' *De schematibus et tropis sacrae scripturae liber* (PL 90:182).

23. Above, chapter 58.

24. The example is taken from the *Rhetorica ad Herennium*.

25. 2 Sam 1:23

26. See the passage quoted above, p. 169, note 145.

27. 1 Cor 13:2

28. 1 Cor 13:4, 5

29. 1 Tim 1:5

30. Cf. Ps 41:6 and Sg 6:11 (V)

31. *Epicurus monachus iratus*: the use of *epicurus* as a noun or adjective, to express a pathological type, is a generalization from the treatment of the Epicurean doctrines in the schools, and the deduction that Epicureans must become the victims of their appetites, and never attain their ends. For a good example of this teaching see the last two chapters of John of Salisbury's *Policraticus* (ed. Webb, 2: 412, 418); also the editor's index of proper names, s.v. *Epicurus* (2: 447b).

32. Mt 5:9

33. *Coccus bis tinctus*, or *coccus* alone, scarlet, is frequently used of vestments in the Scriptures, especially in Exodus. Cf. Ex 25:4; Rev 18:16; and, for the artificer, Si 45:13. By a confusion or play with *coccinum* or *cottinum*, the phrase is associated here with a fine undergarment, conveying an implication of saintliness within: *formam uite . . . subornauit*. See Ducange, *Glossarium*, s.v. *coccinum*, quoting The Life of Saint Matilda.

TITLES LISTINGS

MONASTIC STUDIES

Community & Abbot in the Rule of St Benedict I - II
(Adalbert De Vogüé)
Beatrice of Nazareth in Her Context (Roger De Ganck)
Consider Your Call: A Theology of the Monastic Life
(Daniel Rees et al.)
The Finances of the Cistercian Order in the Fourteenth
Century (Peter King)
Fountains Abbey & Its Benefactors (Joan Wardrop)
The Hermit Monks of Grandmont
(Carole A. Hutchison)
In the Unity of the Holy Spirit (Sighard Kleiner)
Monastic Practices (Charles Cummings)
The Occupation of Celtic Sites in Ireland by the Canons
Regular of St Augustine and the Cistercians
(Geraldine Carville)
Reading Saint Benedict (Adalbert de Vogüé)
The Rule of St Benedict: A Doctrinal and Spiritual
Commentary (Adalbert de Vogüé)
The Rule of St Benedict (Br. Pinocchio)
Towards Unification with God (Beatrice of Nazareth
in Her Context, II)
St Hugh of Lincoln (D.H. Farmer)
Serving God First (Sighard Kleiner)
The Way of Silent Love
With Greater Liberty: A Short History of Christian
Monasticism and Religious Orders

CISTERCIAN STUDIES

A Difficult Saint (B. McGuire)
A Second Look at Saint Bernard (J. Leclercq)
Bernard of Clairvaux and the Cistercian Spirit
(Jean Leclercq)
Bernard of Clairvaux: Man, Monk, Mystic
(M. Casey) Tapes and readings
Bernard of Clairvaux: Studies Presented to Dom
Jean Leclercq
Bernardus Magister
Christ the Way: The Christology of Guerric of Igny
(John Morson)
Cistercian Sign Language
The Cistercian Spirit
The Cistercians in Denmark (Brian McGuire)
The Cistercians in Scandinavia (James France)
The Eleventh-century Background of Cîteaux
(Bede K. Lackner)
The Golden Chain: Theological Anthropology of
Isaac of Stella (Bernard McGinn)
Image and Likeness: The Augustinian Spirituality
of William of St Thierry (D.N. Bell)
An Index of Cistercian Works and Authors in the
Libraries of Great Britain I (D.N. Bell)
An Index of Cistercian Authors and Works in Medieval
Library Catalogues in Great Britain (D.N. Bell)
The Mystical Theology of St Bernard (Etiénne Gilson)
Nicolas Cotheret's Annals of Cîteaux (Louis J. Lekai)
The Spiritual Teachings of St Bernard of Clairvaux
(J.R. Sommerfeldt)
Studiosorum Speculum
Wholly Animals: A Book of Beastly Tales (D.N. Bell)
William, Abbot of St Thierry
Women and St Bernard of Clairvaux (Jean Leclercq)

MEDIEVAL RELIGIOUS WOMEN

Lillian Thomas Shank and John A. Nichols, editors

Distant Echoes
Peace Weavers
Hidden Springs: Cistercian Monastic Women

STUDIES IN CISTERCIAN ART AND
ARCHITECTURE

Meredith Parsons Lillich, editor

Volumes I, II, III, IV now available

THOMAS MERTON

The Climate of Monastic Prayer (T. Merton)
The Legacy of Thomas Merton (P. Hart)
The Message of Thomas Merton (P. Hart)
Thomas Merton: The Monastic Journey
Thomas Merton Monk (P.Hart)
Thomas Merton Monk & Artist (Victor Kramer)
Thomas Merton on St Bernard
Toward an Integrated Humanity (M. Basil
Pennington et al.)

CISTERCIAN LITURGICAL
DOCUMENTS SERIES

Chrysogonus Waddell, ocso, editor

Hymn Collection of the Abbey of the Paraclete
Institutiones nostrae: The Paraclete Statutes
Molesme Summer-Season Breviary (4 volumes)
Old French Ordinary and Breviary of the Abbey of
the Paraclete: Text & Commentary (2 vol.)
The Cadouin Breviary (two volumes)
The Twelfth-century Cistercian Psalter
The Twelfth-century Usages of the Cistercian Lay-
brothers
Two Early *Libelli Missarum*

STUDIA PATRISTICA

*Papers of the 1983 Oxford patristics conference
edited by Elizabeth A. Livingstone*

XVIII/I Historica-Gnostica-Biblica
XVIII/2 Critica-Classica-Ascetica-Liturgica
XVIII/3 Second Century-Clement & Origen-
Cappodician Fathers
XVIII/4 *available from Peeters, Leuven*

Cistercian Publications is a non-profit corporation. Its
publishing program is restricted to monastic texts in
translation and books on the monastic tradition.

*North American customers may order these books
through booksellers or directly from the warehouse:*
Cistercian Publications (Distributor)
St Joseph's Abbey
Spencer, Massachusetts 01562
tel: (508) 885-7011 ❖   fax: (508)-885-4687

*Editorial queries and advance book information
should be directed to the Editorial Offices:*
Cistercian Publications
Institute of Cistercian Studies
Western Michigan University
Kalamazoo, Michigan 49008
tel: (616) 387-8920 ❖   fax: (616)-387-8921

A complete catalogue of texts in translation and studies on early, medieval, and modern monasticism is
available at no cost from Cistercian Publications.

CISTERCIAN TEXTS

THE WORKS OF
BERNARD OF CLAIRVAUX

Apologia to Abbot William
Five Books on Consideration: Advice to a Pope
Grace and Free Choice
Homilies in Praise of the Blessed Virgin Mary
The Life and Death of Saint Malachy the Irishman
Love without Measure. Extracts from the Writings
    of St Bernard (Paul Dimier)
On Loving God
The Parables of Saint Bernard (Michael Casey)
Sermons for the Summer Season
Sermons on the Song of Songs I - IV
The Steps of Humility and Pride

THE WORKS OF
WILLIAM OF SAINT THIERRY

The Enigma of Faith
Exposition on the Epistle to the Romans
Exposition on the Song of Songs
The Golden Epistle
The Nature of Dignity of Love

THE WORKS OF AELRED OF RIEVAULX

Dialogue on the Soul
The Life of Aelred of Rievaulx by Walter Daniel
The Mirror of Charity
Spiritual Friendship
Treatises I: On Jesus at the Age of Twelve, Rule for
    a Recluse, The Pastoral Prayer

THE WORKS OF JOHN OF FORD

Sermons on the Final Verses of the Songs of Songs I - VII

THE WORKS OF GILBERT OF HOYLAND

Sermons on the Songs of Songs I-III
Treatises, Sermons and Epistles

OTHER EARLY CISTERCIAN WRITERS

The Letters of Adam of Perseigne I
Baldwin of Ford: Spiritual Tractates I - II
Gertrud the Great of Helfta: Spiritual Exercises
Gertrud the Great of Helfta: The Herald of God's
    Loving-Kindness
Guerric of Igny: Liturgical Sermons I - II
Idung of Prüfening: Cistercians and Cluniacs: The
    Case of Cîteaux
Isaac of Stella: Sermons on the Christian Year
The Life of Beatrice of Nazareth
Serlo of Wilton & Serlo of Savigny
Stephen of Lexington: Letters from Ireland
Stephen of Sawley: Treatises

MONASTIC TEXTS

EASTERN CHRISTIAN TRADITION

Besa: The Life of Shenoute
Cyril of Scythopolis: Lives of the Monks of Palestine

Dorotheos of Gaza: Discourses
Evagrius Ponticus:Praktikos and Chapters on Prayer
The Harlots of the Desert (Benedicta Ward)
John Moschos: The Spiritual Meadow
Iosif Volotsky: Monastic Rule
The Lives of the Desert Fathers
The Lives of Simeon Stylites (Robert Doran)
The Luminous Eye (Sebastian Brock)
The Meditations of Guigo, Prior of the Chaterhouse
    (A. Gordon Mursell)
Mena of Nikiou: Isaac of Alexandria & St Macrobius
Pachomian Koinonia I - III
Paphnutius: A Histories of the Monks of Upper Egypt
The Sayings of the Desert Fathers
Spiritual Direction in the Early Christian East (Irénée
    Hausherr)
Symeon the New Theologian: The Theological and
       Practical Treatises & The Three Theological
       Discourses
The Syriac Fathers on Prayer and the Spiritual Life
    (Sebastian Brock)
The Wound of Love: A Carthusian Miscellany

WESTERN CHRISTIAN TRADITION

Anselm of Canterbury: Letters I - III
Bede: Commentary on the Seven Catholic Epistles
Bede: Commentary on the Acts of the Apostles
Bede: Homilies on the Gospels I - II
Conferences of John Cassian, I - III
Gregory the Great: Forty Gospel Homilies
Guigo II the Carthusian: Ladder of Monks and
    Twelve Meditations
Handmaids of the Lord: The Lives of Holy Women in
    Late Antiquity and the Early Middle Ages (Joan
    Petersen)
Peter of Celle: Selected Works
The Letters of Armand-Jean de Rancé I - II
The Rule of the Master

CHRISTIAN SPIRITUALITY

Abba: Guides to Wholeness & Holiness East & West
A Cloud of Witnesses: The Development of
    Christian Doctrine (D.N. Bell)
Athirst for God: Spiritual Desire in Bernard of
    Clairvaux's Sermons on the Song of Songs
    (M. Casey)
Cistercian Way (André Louf)
Drinking From the Hidden Fountain (Spidlék)
Eros and Allegory: Medieval Exegesis of the Song of
    Songs (Denys Turner)
Fathers Talking (Aelred Squire)
Friendship and Community (B. McGuire)
From Cloister to Classroom
Herald of Unity: The Life of Maria Gabrielle
    Sagheddu (M. Driscoll)
Life of St Mary Magdalene and of Her Sister
    St Martha (D. Mycoff)
The Name of Jesus (Irénée Hausherr)
No Moment Too Small (Norvene Vest)
Penthos: The Doctrine of Compunction in the
    Christian East (Irénée Hausherr)
Rancé and the Trappist Legacy (A.J. Krailsheimer)
The Roots of the Modern Christian Tradition
Russian Mystics (S. Bolshakoff)
The Spirituality of the Christian East (Tomas Spidlik)
Spirituality of the Medieval West (André Vauchez)
Tuning In To Grace (André Louf)